Project Management For Beginners

A Powerful System For Managing Projects, Planning, Organizing & Scheduling Work & Life - With Proven Productivity, Leadership & Procrastination Hacks To Get More Done

Russell Barlow

All Rights.Reserved.

Table of Contents

INTRODUCTION 1

CHAPTER ONE : PROJECT MANAGEMENT AT A GLANCE (PRE & POST HISTORICAL BACKGROUND) 5

CHAPTER TWO : PROJECT MANAGEMENT (DEFINITIONS AND CONCEPTS) 16

CHAPTER THREE : PROJECT MANAGEMENT (HOW TO BEGIN) 26

CHAPTER FOUR : THE PROJECT MANAGER 39

CHAPTER FIVE : HOW TO BE A SUCCESSFUL PROJECT MANAGER 50

CHAPTER SIX : COMMON MISTAKES YOU WOULD ENCOUNTER AS A BEGINNER 63

CHAPTER SEVEN : NEW TRENDS IN PROJECT MANAGEMENT 75

CHAPTER EIGHT : PROJECT PLANNING 87

CHAPTER NINE : PROJECT CONTROL 99

CHAPTER TEN : KEY TECHNIQUES, METHODOLOGIES, AND TOOLS OF PROJECT MANAGEMENT 111

CHAPTER ELEVEN : COMMON RISKS AND THEIR CONTROL. 126

CHAPTER TWELVE : TAPPING INTO THE REALM
OF POSSIBILITIES 133

CONCLUSION 139

Introduction

To begin with, planning an event, a process or even a simple step is something that is synonymous to our everyday lifestyle. As the saying goes, he who fails to plan will definitely plan to fail; thus, the need for having careful and strategic planning and execution of our daily activities no matter how little or insignificant they might turn out to be. Now, this brings us to the world of Project Management.

Additionally, the paradigm shift in the organizational and professional side of the world today has called for a whole new dimension as regards effective and efficient output. Lots of companies, organizations, firms, and so much more now focus their lens on the effective planning process in order to achieve more within the shortest time. And no matter how well we turn this, Project Management seems to be the only available option here. Thus, the need for Project Managers.

Be that as it may, if there is a high rise of people rushing into Project Management as a result of this paradigm shift, then we can say there are going to be a whole bunch of ignorant and inexperienced people that would definitely find themselves in the world of Project Management for the first time in their life; thus, the need for this book.

I'm very sure most of you are familiar with these two words – Project Management. While some must have undergone a professional course on it, others might have read a thing or two about it online. Some might not even have the faintest idea about the words altogether. Nevertheless, this book will keep you abreast with the world of Project Management and how you all can infuse it in your daily life.

Do you find it very hard in organizing, planning, and executing a project, a simple task or even a daily activity no matter how hard you try? Do you find it hard to relate and work hand in hand with others in order to come up with an amazing result? Do you find it almost impossible to stay consistent in your line of work or business, thereby, leading to fluctuations in your success rate and inconsistencies?

Well, not to worry, this book would enlighten you on these individual aspects, thereby making sure you turn out even better than the way you were before picking it up. It will broaden your horizon in the area of Project Management if ever you've had an idea on the concepts earlier. It would still go ahead in making you see the recent trends that have taken the forefront of Project Management.

With Project Management, all your days of unbalanced management and planning are over. This book would go a long way in correcting such outcomes and in the end, you will be filled with more than enough confidence while planning and executing. There is no better feeling than knowing exactly what you are doing and having control.

Far from planning and executing, there are other key areas you would never find in most Project Management books and contents out there. All these important but rare segments and areas are well explained in the chapters of this book. Additionally, there are practical and real-life questions and answers this book would throw at you. Instead of keeping everything theoretical, this book would take you into the real sense of the world. With practical examples and real-life situations, this book would ensure you fully understand the concept of Project Management.

Be that as it may, all beginners out there are liable to make mistakes in the course of Project Management. When these happen, then I will urge you to stay calm and collected no matter how the situation may be because the solutions to these mistakes might just be right in front of you. This is why we would outline the key mistakes that are quite familiar with beginners. Learn from it and the sky would definitely be your starting point as regards Project Management.

In the end, no one will be able to surpass your Project Management skill, not even those that studied it as a discipline. We are going to mold you from being a beginner to an expert in this field. But till then, why not take a deep breath, relax, and allow us to take you on this exceptional journey into the world of Project Management? Let's get to it, shall we?

Chapter One

Project Management at a Glance (Pre & Post Historical Background)

The rise of Project Management in today's world was a gradual process which saw it skyrocket rocket from the least of the things cherished in the world of professionalism to the top of them all. Ripple by ripple, what had seemed like an ordinary idea conceived many years ago had gained its strong footing in the world as a whole. People now introduce the art of Project Management into whatever they want to do.

For example, Project Management had now become a necessary condition for prospective job seekers before getting employed. Employers also didn't just stay relaxed, they also followed the bandwagon by focusing their attention on this necessary condition. They believe planning before executing is the most important trait one can hold in the professional level, that way, their mind would be at peace whenever they give an employee a task to complete.

Now, this is just a tip of the iceberg as regards what Project Management has to offer. Be that as it may, it is important to know that Project Management in real sense deals with logic, tact, resourcefulness, and creativity. These are attributes even the most boring Project Managers must possess in order to make things work in their favor.

Project Management deals with seeing the other components and parts of a project as an extension or even a combination that makes up the whole. In order words, the different parts that make up your project should be seen as related and important ingredients that would make your project effectively managed. Thus, each unit, section, and the cabinet must be given due attention.

Let's say your whole body is a project and your hands, eyes, nose, legs, chest, toes, and other parts are all different but important units that make up the project. Would you neglect the eyes and focus on other parts? The answer is no. And that is the same way you won't neglect the nose or legs and expect to have a perfect and healthy body. This same instance works perfectly for Project Management.

You can't expect your project to be effectively managed when you don't even give each necessary component the same proportion of attention and care. You really need to make sure these different units and components are adequately managed too. That is the only way you can get a good result in your Project

Management. As a beginner, you might get carried away or overwhelmed by a particular unit in a project and often focus your attention more in it without balancing it with the rest. Now, that is not something bad, especially if you are able to detect this problem sooner. However, if you weren't, then don't beat yourself up about it. Trust me, you can always pick yourself up again and again.

Now, as a beginner, I know you must have been dying to know all about the historical background of this amazing way of getting an effective result and organizing oneself. Also, if you are an expert, it is quite pertinent for you to stay abreast with the historical background of your cherished Project Management. In case you start saying you don't need to know the history or you aren't interested, then, believe me, knowing the history of Project Management would come in handy when the need arises. Additionally, knowing the past would definitely open up our mind for better digestion of the future. In order words, if we know the history of Project Management, we would be able to fully understand and tweak Project Management to our favor.

Historical Background of Project Management

Categorically, we wouldn't be far from the truth if we boldly say that Project Management has been around for like an eternity. Come to think of it, planning, executing, and management is three things that have been quite synonymous to man right from the inception. Even the caveman or the early man would make traps in catching their prey and food. They would create shelter for themselves. Create a fire in time of cold. Now that is what I call planning and management.

What makes theirs different is that the name 'Project Management' hadn't been conceived and instead, 'Survival' was used in place of it. Be that as it may, it's still called Project Management. You can't seriously say because the name wasn't introduced then, thus, it's far from Project Management. Hope you can share the same thought for Apples, Grapes, Blueberries, and so much more.

It is important to know that there had been lots of important, massive, and ancient structures in time which was only possible as a result of proper and adequate management. A very big example is the Egyptian Pyramids. There is no way anyone could pull that off without assembling a group and managing them adequately. Now, that is Project Management at its peak.

Thus, what picture am I trying to draw here? Project Management is real and it had been in existence since the beginning of time. It is not something new as many would have you believe. It is, in fact, one of the oldest ways of making things done effectively and efficiently without wasting resources. Following this amazing work of collective effort, many philosophers and scholars now began attributing and associating the feat with the term, Project Management.

Ripple by ripple, Project Management became codified and also became a discipline which many would come to study. Along the line, many vital points and ideas were propounded as a contribution to the development of this new discipline, Project Management. A very big example is the Gantt Chart and the Agile Manifesto. Ever since its development, it had continued to make a reasonable impact on the lives of many. Though it might be an old process of getting things done, it is still as effective and efficient as ever.

It is important to know that modern day Project Management is very different from the ancient one. While the ancient system of managing projects is said to be crude and rusty but effective, the modern day Project Management is well detailed, well structured, and well organized. Thus, making their foundation and tenets a bit different though still the same in some ways. For example, when the Egyptians built the large pyramids for the Pharaohs, they knew such project would be enormous and takes time, thus, they assembled a large group of people for the task, but not without having someone among them as their manager.

According to the records, each manager and their group of hardworking people were entitled to a pyramid and must be completed within the same time range. These managers showed great enthusiasm, character, and commitment towards the project and ensured they did a great job in the end. Now, those are part of the key attribute you must exude as a great Project Manager.

Furthermore, when the great wall of China was erected, the emperor knew it was no small feat. Thus, there were records that show the intense planning and executing even before the project began. In today's world, one should be sure to plan his or herself beforehand, so as not to be taken unaware or caught off guard as regards any project. If the Old Chinese Empire hadn't planned ahead of time, they wouldn't have been able to complete or even start building the great wall.

Additionally, a large group of people was tasked to complete the project. Ranging from the commoners to the elites, from the criminals to the soldiers, from the young to the old, from the rich to the poor. In total, millions of people were tasked to start and finish up the project and not without station managers placed at every strategic point of the wall. Well there you have it, these are evidence that shows how much of importance Project Management had been over time and how long it had been of existence.

In recent times, everything we do points towards Project Management. Every one of our key industries today needs effective Project Management in order to get things done. From the Manufacturing Industry down to the Construction Industry. Everything boils down to Project Management. When Sir Henry Ford developed his world record assemble system which made his work 10 times faster, he was basically applying the knowledge of Project Management.

When the American states embarked on rehabilitation and reconstruction after the Civil War, Project Management was what helped them in making sure everything was done effectively and efficiently while mincing every resource out there. Project Management goes way beyond discipline, it is a part of us. It is what we do every day of our lives either consciously or unconsciously.

This is why as beginners of this amazing discipline, we should always look beyond the ordinary. That way we would realize that with Project Management, everything around us would definitely take good shape. Notwithstanding, we would definitely find ourselves at the top of every situation; either good or bad. If we look at every situation closely, be it a task, a project, or just normal activity, we would be stunned at the fact that it's either there is a leadership role to be played, a particular budget put in place or a schedule to be met at all cost. However, with Project Management, successful delivery is definitely guaranteed.

Modern Day History

It is important to know that Project Management was coined into its modern form with lots of charts, theories, formulations, and principles introduced at the 1990s. With time, technology started taking a whole new dimension with lots of exciting innovations and inventions being developed by diverse companies all over the world, so also Project Management. In order words, there was a need for the management of these amazing project. Here are some of the few key contributions and ideas of modern-day Project Management;

1. The Principles of Scientific Management: Frederic Taylor was the developer of this principle in his 1911 publication, "The Principles of Scientific Management". In his work, he focused his lens in the steel industry where he hoped to transform the unskilled workers into more complex form by striving hard to learn new and simple techniques. He also mentioned the importance of having incentive-based wage systems out there as well as the general use of time-saving techniques.

2. The Gantt Chart: As a beginner, you would definitely come across this chart as many times as possible. Many believe that the Gantt Chart is the foundation of modern-day Project Management.

Little wonder why they also see Henry Gantt as the father of modern-day Project Management. Be that as it may, the Gantt Chart is an innovative and eponymous diagram which can be said be as effective and efficient as Project Management itself.

According to Gantt himself, he believes that the Gantt Chat would allow you visualize tasks ahead of time and even enable you to link these tasks together. The importance of the Gantt Chart is for one to be able to keep their schedule intact. The Gantt Chart had been used in executing top projects all over the world since its introduction. For example, the Hoover Dam built in 1931. In recent times, it has even shifted it's focus and attention in the digital world as it now comes in online versions.

3. The American Association of Cost Engineers: Before going international, the American Association of Cost Engineers was previously created by a group of like-minded individuals who are specialists in the field of Project Management. They are mainly concerned with planning, executing, cost estimating, and so much more. Currently, it is one of the most powerful bodies in the world of Project Management.

4. The Critical Path: Ever heard of this outstanding

technique? I'm sure you haven't. As a beginner, this type of technique will sound foreign to your ears and that is very normal. As you begin to move from the beginner stage to being an expert, you would now start getting familiar with such technique. Now, what does the Critical Path does? It is an effective technique used to measure the time frame of a project.

In case you want to know how long a particular project would take so as to adequately prepare for it, then this is the right technique for you. As developed by Dupont in 1957, the technique would examine the sequence of activities that has the lowest level of scheduling flexibility. That way, you would get an appropriate time frame.

5. The International Project Management Association: As one of the world earliest Project Management associations, the International Project Management Association was created in 1965 in Vienna. When it was first created, it was with the motive of allowing Project Managers all around the globe to connect and share ideas under one umbrella. Right now, the International Project Management Association consists of 50 national and internationally recognized Project Management associations and organizations. It had also moved from Vienna to Switzerland and

has over 150,000 worthy members from all over the globe.

In order to understand a particular subject matter, it is important for us to first understand its history. History is the vehicle that transports today and tomorrow. Thus, the need for us to revisit the beginnings of Project Management and how it was conceived. This would further shed more light on the concept of Project Management. Be that as it may, this book will take you even deeper. It will help connect your everyday life with Project Management and how you can further improve it with this concept. Want to find out about this? Then follow us to the next chapters.

Chapter Two

Project Management (Definitions and Concepts)

Project Management is a trending topic in recent times with a whole lot of people delving into this line of discipline. Little by little, it had become significant in both our professional world and our personal affairs. Just as the name entails, Project Management simply deals with the art of managing projects as they come. When you successfully handle projects to their efficiently and effectively, you are said to be a good Project Manager. It doesn't necessarily mean one would have a degree or certificate in it before qualifying for the position.

It is pertinent to know that some people have these outstanding skills inherent in them. To them, it's more like inborn skills which they got from birth. Even without learning, reading, or even practicing Project Management, they find themselves extremely good at it. Yes, such people do exist. Nevertheless, if you don't find yourself in such a category, then I guess this is why you are here in the first place. This is why you are picking up this book, so as to brush your crude skills and elevate you from being a beginner to an expert.

Over the past many decades, Project Management had been defined by lots of scholars of the field or discipline and each definition are popularly acceptable. This chapter would help familiarize you with these concise definitions and concept, so as to give you a good idea of what Project Management really is. So the question really is, what does Project Management really entail?

But before we do that, it is important that we know what Project is all about. We can't possibly delve into Project Management without knowing what a Project is all about. When you call yourself a Manager, then there must certainly be something you are managing. This is practically called a project. Anything that has a beginning and an end are a Project. A Project doesn't really have to be something tangible or even official.

A Project is a well-collected effort which consists of basically different parts of a group directed towards a particular goal. According to the PMBOK (Project Management Body of Knowledge) 3rd edition;

"A project is defined as a temporary endeavor with a beginning and an end and it must be used to create a unique product, service or result. Further, it is progressively elaborated. What this definition of a project means is that projects are those activities that cannot go on indefinitely and must have a defined purpose."

With that being said, we can now discuss what Project Management really entails. We aren't farfetched from the truth if we say that Project Management is all about the combination of both Project and Management. Project Management is far more than just heading a group of like-minded individuals. It involves tact, commitment, and perseverance.

According to Jack Meredith, Samuel MantelJack R. Meredith, and Samuel J. Mantel, Jr, I quote;

"Project management is in terms of producing project outcomes within the three objectives of cost, schedule, and specifications. Project managers are then expected to develop and execute a project plan that meets cost, schedule, and specification parameters. According to this view, project management is the application of everything a project manager does to meet these parameters. This approach to defining project management shares PMI's focus on the project outcomes in terms of requirements."

According to this definition, Project Management goes beyond directing and planning. It also involves focusing on the cost benefits and effectiveness. One of the qualities of a good Project Manager is the ability to make good use of the available resources, no matter how little it might be. Additionally, the ability of a manager to make sure everything goes according to plan is also paramount.

In another view, Investopedia views Project Management differently. In their defense, they see Project Management as something unique. That way, they see;

"Project management as the planning and organization of a company's resources to move a specific task, event, or duty towards completion. It can involve a one-time project or an ongoing activity, and resources managed include personnel, finances, technology, and intellectual property. Every project usually has a budget and a time frame. Project management keeps everything moving smoothly, on time, and on budget. That means when the planned time frame is coming to an end, the project manager may keep all the team members working on the project to finish on schedule."

According to Desmond Cook (The Nature of Project Management, Working Paper, Ohio State University, 1968), he summarizes the definitions of Baumgartner, Cleland, and Gaddis in terms of the project manager's role;

"To produce a product by integrating professional persons into a team operating within time, cost, and performance parameters with that team operating within some lines of organizational responsibilities and authority." Cook goes on to say that projects have four characteristics. They have a single objective, are usually complex in nature, consist of a series of unique tasks, and are normally a one-of-a-kind or non-repetitive activity."

Be that as it may, I believe you now have your own concise meaning of Project Management. Project Management is not just any activity or endeavor, it far more than that. As a matter of fact, it's a strategic process of organizing, planning, scheduling, and even directed to the achievement of one goal – success.

When you see those topnotch companies out there making waves and coming out with a whole new idea, then it's definitely because of their advance and outstanding Project Management team. A weak Project Management team in a company mostly leads to the downfall of that company. Project Management is a very important section of a company. You don't expect the account section to double up as the Project Management team, right? The same way you don't expect the janitors to plan and execute the projects of a company. Thus, the need for Project Management in every company, organization or firm.

Aside from these definitions, this chapter would also look into the important concepts associated with Project Management. On a brief note, we would equip you with these concepts that way, you will be able to fully grasp the real meaning of Project Management as a whole. These concepts are quite numerous but we will only limit ourselves to the few important concepts of Project Management. They are as follows;

1. Planning: This is one of the most important concepts in Project Management. Before executing any project, one must first go back to the drawing board and strategize how to go about it. When we plan, we are basically going to achieve success no matter how shrewd the situation or project might turn out to be. Planning is all about mapping out, drawing out, and giving cognizance to a strategic position that would enable you to achieve success in your endeavors.

   All scholars of this discipline (Project Management) had reached an agreement on the important role planning plays in managing a project. Imagine a Manager going about directing and executing projects without even a plan? That would be disastrous, isn't it? Additionally, for one to be a good leader, he or she must be very good at planning. When you have everything mapped out already, people will be obliged to follow you, especially when they know there is a well-detailed plan that would enhance their success.

   Additionally, planning in Project Management

is what had shot up the topnotch organizations of the world today. Even in our personal lives, when we plan ourselves adequately and appropriately, we would realize that things would start taking shape in our lives. We would realize that everything will start looking up and when they don't, there will be no cause for alarm because we must have already made a plan for such an occasion.

We would discuss the term Project Planning further in the course of this book. That way, we would be able to touch every vital part of planning in Project Management. Be that as it may, planning is a concept we can't do without in this line of discipline. As a matter of fact, when we hear the term Project Management, the next thing that comes to our mind is planning. In order words, how we can use planning in making sure our projects are effectively managed.

2. Scheduling: This is also another great concept as regards Project Management. One of the outstanding qualities that make a very good Project Manager is the ability to tell correct schedules and also to keep to it. If we can uphold our Project Schedules, then we would be able to maintain and minimize the use of resources available for that project. In Project Management, Scheduling is a key concept that was developed

and aided with the Gantt Chart and the Critical Path.

It became so important that a lot of Project Managers out there would rather stick focus their lens of the concept in managing their project so as to minimize the resources to be used and also to maximize profits that will be accrued from it. Scheduling gained lots of attention in Project Management when Dupont made a profit of over a million dollars after following the Critical Path technique in predicting correct schedules of his projects. This saved him from unnecessary spending, planning, and so much more.

3. Management: Project Management is all about being a good manager. When you have the ability to make good use of the resources available no matter how little, towards the success of a project, then you can parade yourself as a good Project Manager. As a good manager, the first thing you should be able to do when you are faced with a project is to make sure things everything is in order. And when I mean everything, I'm talking about the machinery, the resources, the manpower, and so much more.

As a concept of Project Management, the ability to manage a project to its desired outcome or destination lies solely with the capability of the management. If the management is weak, poor, and unorganized, then the project would definitely fall apart. In order words, everything that was set to be achieved would not be entirely possible. Be that as it may, in as much as the management is an important concept in Project Management, other concepts are equally as important. One wouldn't be farfetched from the truth if he or she ends up saying these concepts are what makes up a successful Project Manager.

Furthermore, if you want to become successful in this field or discipline, then you need to know the right set of people that would benefit and move your project forward in no time. As a manager, it is your responsibility to hire the right set of people for the job. There should be no emotional attachment when managing a project. Everything should be strictly professional. Thus, good management begets a good project outcome.

4. Control: If you are a Project Manager or vast in the area of Project Management, then you should know that Control is a concept you shouldn't joke with. In the Old Chinese Empire, the head of their projects wield amazing and overwhelming power, that way, he was able to control others other him and get the job done in no time. If the builders of the Great Wall of China weren't under the

command of a single head (Project Manager), then what can be said to be a wonder of the world today would have existed.

Now, that is the power of Control in Project Management. It is not just a concept in Project Management but unarguably one of the outstanding qualities a Project Manager must possess. Make sure you are in total control of your project. In the end, the only person to bear the brunt of the outcome either good or bad will be just you. Thus, having control of your team or project is of utmost importance.

Project Management definition and concepts would further sensitize you with the topic. You will be shocked to know that what you know as the definition of Project Management is a very wrong definition. Things like that happen every day of our lives. With every day that passes, we will learn new things. Thus, I believe this chapter had taught you something new. However, you haven't seen anything yet. Turn the page over and enjoy our next chapter as it promises to be more interesting.

Chapter Three

Project Management (How to begin)

In our previous chapters, we looked into the historical origin (pre and post-historical days) of Project Management and also highlighted the important concepts associated with the discipline. This is solely to keep you abreast and enlightened on the subject matter before finally delving into it. We can't really learn about something new without fully understanding its history. In other words, we can't fully know about something without tracing its root. This is because knowing the history would only give us a better understanding of what that thing really is.

Now, as a beginner, you might be wondering how to go about becoming a good Project Manager overnight. You might also be wondering how much difficulty one must cross before becoming an expert in this discipline. Well sorry to burst your bubbles, Project Management is not really as difficult as others have painted it. It is in fact very easy and can be easily understood if only you would set your mind at excelling in it. Remember, we can only become who and what we want to be if only we learn to believe in ourselves.

Ask yourself these important questions. How did Bill Gates become one of the richest men alive? If Project Management is so difficult as many had painted it, how then did some people get to possess the trait even without learning or studying it? Funny right? If some of us don't even get to drop a sweat before becoming an exceptional Project Manager, why then would you imagine yourself flopping at it? This chapter would enlighten you on the possible ways to start becoming a good Project Manager. It would show you how to start learning Project Management and equipping yourself with the amazing trait in no time.

Trust me, Project Management might sound sophisticated, it is one of the simplest things you would ever learn. Having a clear understanding of Project Management would require the possession of certain qualities and skills. For beginners, you need to first make up your mind and reach a decision on Project Management itself. How badly do you want to be a Project Manager? Are you willing to make compromises and necessary sacrifices when the need arises? Are you willing to learn patiently and attentively? If your answer to these questions is a yes, then there is nothing stopping you from becoming a good Project Manager.

Project Management goes beyond being the head of management or team. In fact, it entails something even more. It encompasses the abilities to manage schedules and deadlines appropriately. It focuses on having a perfect understanding of what the project really entails and possessing the skills to encourage, motivate, and lift the morale of your fellow teammates. Mind you, a good Project Manager must have the ability to sing the praises of his or her team members when the need arises. In order words, you should be able to build a good working relationship with your team.

Additionally, your analytical and budget making skills must be topnotch. When you learn the art of Project Management, these are the likely qualities you would eventually possess at the end of the day. Quite amazing, isn't it? Imagine having all these abilities combine in your perfect little body, you will be formidable at work. You will be able to achieve progress even without trying hard and above all, people will definitely like to associate themselves with you.

Be that as it may, it is important to know that you being the head of a project (Project Manager) don't necessarily make you the ultimate success of that project. It doesn't mean you alone hold the keys to the success of the project. A lot of us out there end up allowing our rate of success gets to our head thereby, we will start thinking the team can't do without us. Remember, no one is irreplaceable. Sooner or later, a perfect replacement for you will definitely come by. Thus, stay humble. Humility is one of the outstanding traits a Project Manager must possess.

Now that you have made up your mind which is the first step, the next thing you should do is to decide on which way you want to go about being an expert in the field of Project Management. It is important to know that there are many ways in which one can end up being a good Project Manager. Like we had mentioned in our first chapter, Project Management is a trending subject matter that had gained momentum over the last few decades.

Thus, there had been lots of amazing and outstanding efforts by lots of people to perfect and reshape it knowledge acquisition process, thereby, making it easy for people to learn, practice, and understand the art of Project Management. Having said that, there is more than one pathway in which one can become an amazing Project Manager. It would interest you to know that all these means are quite reliable and trusted.

Becoming a Project Manager solely lies on your level of reasoning. At one point in our lives, we all wanted to be one thing or the other. At the age of 10, I wanted to become a doctor. At 15, I saw an aviation-related movie at the cinema and wanted to become a pilot. Now, I'm an influencer, a poet, and a writer. Funny right? Being a writer doesn't stop me from yearning to be a Project Manager. If it doesn't stop me, then I believe it should definitely not be a problem for you either, if truly you want to be a Project Manager. It all depends on how badly we want to be involved in the field of Project Management.

Now, what are these possible ways of becoming a good Project Manager? I'll tell you! First, you can learn the tricks and art of Project Management via extensive self-study. Instead of paying a tutor to take you on the subject matter, how about getting the necessary books and start reading? If you read occasionally about anything, then it's only a matter of time before we get extremely good at that thing. If you read occasionally about Project Management, you will definitely be as good as someone who pays to be tutored. That is if you are not even better.

I once wrote a book on the stock market some time ago. But before writing this book, I made sure I read lots of books about the subject matter – Stock Market. It got to a point that I became so vast, good, and knowledgeable about the old and recent trends of the Stock Market. If you don't know any better, you would say I'm a Stock Broker or I own stock. This is the same outcome you would get when you read extensively about Project Management. You will become your own self-qualified and self-trained Project Manager.

Secondly, you can also choose to study Project Management as a discipline in the varsity. This is, in fact, a very good path to follow as regards learning and becoming a good Project Manager. There are lots of advantages attached to this method of learning Project Management. Someone who studies Project Management tends to be much more vast and knowledgeable than someone who depends on self-study. For example, there might be certain terminologies and concepts which can be quite ambiguous and needed to be explained before assimilating, someone who is studying Project Management as a discipline would have the opportunity to meet with his or her tutor for an explanation while someone who is into self-study might not have the same opportunity.

Additionally, at the end of the study comes certification. Studying Project Management in the varsity comes with this benefit. You will be automatically certified at the end of your study, unlike an extensive self-study where there is no certification whatsoever. Thirdly, some of us might need Project Management as additional experience and certification needed in the line of our jobs. This would serve as an added advantage and shoot us up even higher when being paired with our mates.

Thus, all we need to do is to get an institution or establishment where they offer short time classes on Project Management with a certification at the end of the session. This is another pathway in which we can follow in becoming a good Project Management. When you find yourself in a position where many of the qualities and responsibilities resemble that of a Project Manager, then I believe you know what to do.

Nevertheless, the pathway towards becoming a good Project Manager can be quite difficult for some people and sometimes, it can get very easy too for others. It all depends on a number of factors and how well we play our part in this exciting journey. For example, you don't expect to have a stress-free journey into the field of Project Management if you don't even have time to either read or attend Project Management classes. As simple as I might have painted Project Management at the beginning of this book, if you don't take it seriously, then I'm afraid the road towards achieving success in it wouldn't be as easy as it may be.

You need to be serious with it. You need to make sure you truly and perfectly understand Project Management in its raw form. If Project Management is just about heading a group of people, then every Tom, Dick, and Harry would have been a great Project Manager today. You can choose to make your journey towards becoming an exceptional Project Manager a very long one or just a few steps away. It all lies on your hands completely.

Be that as it may, the next process left for you is to take the bull by the horn. Now that you have made up your mind and also selected how to go about becoming a good Project Manager, then I'll suggest you just get to it without wasting your time any further. Mind you, Project Management might sound easy but I never said you won't experience a setback on this exciting journey. Have you considered the financial aspect of it? Have you considered the time frame? Have you considered other temporary setbacks?

If you are faced with financial challenges, then I'll suggest you stick to the first pathway we mentioned above – Self-Study. With technological improvement here and there, you can now download book related to Project Management on your phones and other gadgets without paying a dime in return. That way, you will be able to keep getting more knowledge on Project Management without even paying for it. This is the safest and cheapest way to go about becoming a good Project Manager.

And as regards the time frame challenges, you really need to be certain if you have time on your hands. I have seen lots of cases where people end up registering for Project Management classes and end up getting preoccupied with work and other activities in return. This happens all the time, thus, we need to be certain before entering into it. As the saying goes, always look before you leap. In the absence of all these challenges you might face, then I'll suggest you just Do It!

But before actually doing it, it is important to know that there are two types of certification as regards

Project Management. We have the Certified Associate in Project Management (CAPM) and also the Project Management Professional (PMP) certification. Now, the choice is entirely yours on which type of certification you would like to acquire at the end of the day. Additionally, both certification is also awarded and offered as a course by the almighty Project Management Institute (PMI).

I know what your questions would be next after reading through these few pines above. What is the difference, right? I knew that would definitely cross our mind. However, asking questions about what you don't know is a very good thing entirely. As the saying goes, he who asks for directions never loses his way! Thanks to Google Map, asking for directions are quite outdated (laughs), just kidding. Let's get back to it, shall we?

Remember we discussed why people acquire this Project Management knowledge and skills above. If you still recall, I made an example of a working individual that needed Project Management skills as part of his new functions and also an individual that just wants to study it with lots of time on his side. That is the difference between both certifications. Where one is strictly for those that have more than enough time to spare for reading, classes, experiences, and so much more, the other is just for those willing to get the certificate without going through much stress.

In order words, where PMP requires lots of prerequisites that would give you a hard time and perfectly mold you into one of the best Project Managers out there, the CAPM certification is also there to give you just the accreditation and certification you badly needed without getting to put in much work. Although both of them require you to take classes, read the books, and finally sit for an exam at the end of the session. I believe you now know the difference between both.

Time is the key factor that differentiates both certifications. Now how do you qualify for these different certifications? It's pretty simple. For the PMP certification, there are basically two types of prerequisites which we can choose from. For advanced learners, you can go for the first type of prerequisite which needs at least more than 4,000 hours of working experience and a degree. The other type of prerequisite is for those of a lower set. If you have a secondary education and at least 4 good years of working experience, then you are good to go.

By now, I believe you should know your strength and weaknesses. I believe you should now be able to choose which prerequisite fits your time frame and qualification. That way, you will be able to choose which certification you would want to pursue. There are examples of people who want the PMP certificate but aren't qualified for it, thus, opted for the CAPM which fits their range and specification at the moment. If you fall into this category, then doing that isn't something bad.

You can, in fact, own both certifications if you want. There is absolutely nothing stopping you from doing that. If you aren't qualified for the PMP maybe because of your limited working experience or your qualifications, then I will suggest you go for the lesser category. Start from there. When you attain that certificate, then you can move to the next. It would even give you more experience than any other person out there. It would be like combining both experiences and certificate, which would definitely be an advantage to you in the long run. Project Management is all about leaving the project in the hands of someone capable. Now, what other capable hands can beat yours?

Lastly, maintaining certification comes next. As a certified owner of the CAPM certificate, there are certain exams you would have to sit for every five years or so, just to maintain the certificate. Additionally, it is important to know that these exams can take any form as they change with time, thus, we would advise you to really prepare yourself before going into the exam hall.

And for PMP certificate holders, the maintenance of their certificates takes a whole new dimension entirely. Instead of writing an exam like the CAPM, you will have to make sure you must have completed at least 60 professional development units (PDUs) year in, year out. Now, the question is how do you go about earning these units? It's simple but quite hard at the same time. All you need to do is to make sure you stay active in the world of Project Management or something related to it by running other related courses, either online or in person, going out there to give presentations, dishing out your Project Management skills either as a volunteer or on contract, and so much more.

The real reason for the creation of these PDUs is for you to keep developing and progressing as a Project Manager. I believe if you continue to focus on your Project Management skills without being stagnant, then there will be room for improvement every now and then. That is all you need to know before starting out your Project Management career. The rest is for you to go out there and take the world by storm. Always find the time to learn something new. Also, don't forget to incorporate your experience with everyday endeavors.

Remember, Project Management is not just for our professional use but also our personal lives. You can borrow some of the skills and arrange your life in an orderly manner. You can even help your family and friends out in a time of need. You can help them take control whenever you feel they had lost it. As a Project Management expert, even human beings can be a project in the long run. They can be managed effectively and efficiently.

Now, this is the short and long run of how to go about becoming a Project Manager. And if you are already a Project Manager, then you can still improve yourself with this book. Remember, no knowledge is a waste. No matter how vast you think you might be, there are still certain things you don't know and this book would gladly turn your attention to it. Thus, enjoy every bit of it.

Chapter Four

The Project Manager

The Project Manager is a part of the whole that makes the team. A Project Manager is someone that makes the team functions appropriately and adequately. Everything around us is a project, it all depends on how we view it. Be it a personal affair or a professional one, we all need to be tactful and skillful in order to be able to manage that affair effectively and efficiently. For example, in a family situation where an even comes up and the whole family is expected to come together in order to successfully organize something amazing, someone needs to come out as the head of that organizing committee. Tell me, what better person would be perfect for the job other than someone with experience and certification in Project Management?

You will be shocked at how everyone's eyes will suddenly shift to your direction when the need arises. There would be a need for someone to be in charge and that responsibility will definitely rest on your shoulders. That is the power of a Project Manager. A Project Manager is someone who possesses the ability, skill, and experience to successfully motivate, oversee, and control a certain project to its desired destination – that is its success.

A Project Manager position doesn't necessarily mean someone must possess the CAPM and PMP certification. It also doesn't mean someone must be bossy and too confident. As a matter of fact, a good Project Manager should know that he exists for the group, just as the group exists for him or her. In as much as holding a Project Management certificate writes your name in paint in the field of Project Management, not holding one doesn't make you less of a Project Manager either.

It is important to know that a good Project Manager carries the team along. When the Old Egypt built huge and enormous pyramids for their Pharaohs, it wasn't an individual effort. Instead, it was a collective effort which comprises of the bottom-top hierarchy. The whole chain of command (from the Project Managers to the menial workers) had to digest every possible idea and details together and even relate these ideas amongst themselves. Without this necessary cooperation between the team, who knows if the great pyramid might have collapsed on their head while building it?

Also, in some instances, a Project Manager needs to be confident and sometimes resolute in his or her decisions. If a Project Manager doesn't have a mind of his or her own, then there will be no control in the team. On the other hand, control is an important concept a Project Management. It is a concept the Project Manager cannot afford to lose. Always learn to stand on your words and be confident if you are right or things aren't going your way. You should also cultivate the mind of welcoming new exciting ideas from your team. Your team is like your family, treat them as such.

Categorically, we can boldly say that a Project Manager is a professional in the world of Project Management. At least tons of them have a certificate to show for it. As a professional in a particular field, you are joined with the responsibilities and functions of making good and suitable plans, making procurement of any kind, executing a project to the best of your abilities while following a specific and already designed scope and schedule. If you have any problems with mismanagement and other discrepancies in your organization, then before it gets out of hand, I'll recommend you give Project Managers a chance to fix the mess.

They are not only good at making things flourish, but they are also great at making sure everything falls into place without exceeding the time frame. This is their specialty and what they are trained for. You won't find a Project Manager doing the heavy task in a project, neither will you find him participate fully in the running of the organization. Rather, he will be at the forefront, watching every move with his keen eyes and at the same time making the necessary corrections if the need arises. The Project Manager would oversee the whole operation and steer it to success.

And in cases where the project had attained success and progress, the Project Manager would help improve and even maintain this progress even better. The Project Manager will also strive to keep the mutual interaction between various parties in his team. A peaceful Project team will definitely equate to a high chance of successful outcome. That way, the rate at which the project will fail will be extremely low and there would be a maximization of profits, costs, and benefits.

It is also important to know that the praise gotten from the success of a project would mainly go to the Project Manager and the brunt will also be felt by the Project Manager also. It goes both ways. He or she is entirely responsible for the success or failure of the project. Little wonder why some Project Manager goes the extra length in making sure their projects are indeed a success.

Damian used to be a Project Manager for 30 years before he retired and decides to spend the rest of his life with his lovely wife, Beatrice. In an interview with Damian, he continuously stresses out the fact that during his Project Management days, he would go extra length anytime he feels his project is in jeopardy. According to him, sometimes, he will even stay late in the office trying to crack one or two challenges before the whole team reassembles in the morning.

This is one of the attributes of a Project Manager. Are you getting cold fit already about Project Management? Not to worry, sometimes, the work doesn't even require much stress at all. Sometimes as a Project Manager, you can be very lucky in meeting a group of like-minded individuals in the team. This would even make your work easy. There is also a chance of you meeting difficult people in the course of this work. Trust me, some people can really get on your nerves, especially when they feel threatened or invaded.

Some people can be like that. As a Project Manager, if you are assigned to a new team, there is every tendency that the people of the team would not really be happy and receptive in the beginning. Some might even want you to win their trust. As a Project Manager, you will be taught all this. Thus, you will be more than equipped to face such situations. When that happens, take a deep breath and make sure you take absolute control. Remember, you are the boss.

Additionally, a Project Manager can also double up as the client representative when the need arises. He or she can take action or act on behalf of the client if the occasion warrants it. As a client, if you are not available to take action or decision on a project, then be rest assured that the Project Manager is able and capable of taking appropriate decisions. It is an expertise that is expected of the Project Manager. He or she is expected to take different forms and adapt to the wishes and procedures of the client.

That way, he or she would be able to keep the client happy no matter how difficult the task may be. The goal of every Project Manager is to make sure that the client stays happy no matter what. Thus, he or she should always be up to date as regards the organization's cost, the benefits, the risks, and client satisfaction.

Types of Project Managers

1. Construction Project Manager: This is a very intriguing section of the field of Project Management. It is a section of Project Management that deals solely with construction projects. If you are having issues with the putting together a formidable team to oversee and execute your construction projects, then hiring a professional in the field of Construction Project Management is your best bet

    Currently, there is a valid certification and qualification that had been ruling the world of the American construction industry. Not just anyone can wake up today and claim to be vast in the area of construction project management. Each state also has its own specifications and requirements for becoming one. Be that as it may, a lot of competent people had been disqualified or even barricaded from getting a license, thus, there had been many agitations as regards this unfair treatment.

As a direct response to it, many groups and trade unions have come up with commonly acceptable grounds for all competent construction project management. That way, tests, and exams can be set to determine that. Afterward, the CCM certificate would be issued to you by the Construction Management Association of America (CMAA). That way, you would be able to hold competency and even gain experience.

Additionally, you can now study Construction Management as a degree program at the University. Additionally, there is also a recent development in the colleges today as they now offer Project Management as a master degree course. If you know you already have working experience as regards Project Management, then taking these courses won't be a bad idea. If you have a construction problem, let the Project Managers take care of it.

2. Architectural Project Manager: This type of

Project Managers deal with architectural problems. They are quite vast in the field of architecture. This particular type of Project Management share similarities with the construction Project Management and mostly work hand in hand in making sure the project gets to its final destination and outcome. While the Construction project managers deal with the hard part of the job, Architectural project managers deal with the soft part of the job.

They make sure they focus on the design of the whole project and head the design team. They make an effort in making sure the project goes smoothly and perfectly. They also deal with the issue of budget creation scheduling of the project, and most importantly quality control. These are the core responsibilities of Architectural project managers.

3. Insurance Claim Project Manager: These types of Project Managers deals mainly with the Insurance Industry. They are always at the forefront of keeping the client satisfied. They are extremely good at making sure the client gets the best out of their unfortunate circumstances and situations. They are always in charge of the restorations of the client loss, no matter how much.

4. Engineering Project Manager: Do you know that

there are Project Managers that specializes in the engineering field? They work closely with other departments in the engineering field in order to come out with the right outcome. They will put together a formidable team and oversee the progress closely. If need be, they can be in the field to oversee things themselves. They can as well work hand in hand with different professionals.

5. Software Project Manager: a software project manager is just as important as any other type of project managers out there. Instead of the traditional way of seeing Project Management (Construction and Manufacturing), software management is a whole new phase which is as important and legit as other types of Project Management we have. Just as other Project Management has extensive knowledge in their field, so it the software project managers.

They have a vast amount of knowledge in software development. A lot of them even hold a formal background in the field of computer science, information technology, and so much more. Software Project Managers are highly skilled and extremely amazing at what they do. They are particularly skilled in the field of software Management. If you have a problem with your software or you have a project at hand that needs utmost perfection, then a software manager is your best bet.

Any good and competent software manager is expected to be vast in the area of Software Development Life Cycle (SDLC). Mind you, having this knowledge doesn't come easy. It requires a lot of competence, skill, and knowledge to attain this feat. A good software Project Manager must have at least a PMP certification.

Responsibilities and Duties of a Project Manager

The Project Manager is like the Grand Master of the whole project. He or she is the brain behind the whole project. He or she is the head that makes sure the body works perfectly. Have you ever seen a train without an engine? Or a car without steering? This is who a Project Manager is. When other teammates start slacking off, it is the duty of the Project Manager to shake them up. However, the different type of Project Managers we mentioned above has their own specific functions and duties. Thus, here are the responsibilities of a Project Manager;

6. A Project Manager is faced with the responsibility of coming up with great Project Plans.

7. They also manage project stakeholders.

8. It is their duty to enable good communication amongst the team.

9. They are also faced with the responsibility of managing the whole project team.

10. They also make sure the risks are managed effectively.

11. Project Managers come up with an amazing budget.

12. They try to meet up with the schedule.

13. How about managing conflicts in the team? That is their responsibility.

14. They motivate their other team members.

15. They are faced with Project delivery.

The Project Manager is someone who is extremely intelligent and has at least the slightest idea about every department in a project. From the planning down to the execution, he or she must be actively involved in order to drive the project home. Thus, if you want to be this type of Project Manager, the will implore you to read this chapter over and over again. The next chapter would focus on tips to being a successful Project Manager, you don't want to miss it.

Chapter Five

How to be a Successful Project Manager

I'm sure you are smiling and grinning from teeth to teeth after knowing the amazing and outstanding qualities you would hold when you eventually move from being a beginner to an expert in the world of Project Management. A Project Manager is the Superman of the team. He is the kind of person the whole team looks at for solutions to challenges and problems. Now, imagine being that person. Having so much control and power over others and at the same time enjoying the benefits and support of the people around you. Trust me, no feeling beats such feeling.

To be a Project Manager is very easy. With the little experience and formal background you have, all you need to do is to enroll yourself in the PMI (Project Management Institute) as a student of Project Management. You will also need to take classes and examinations at the end of every session. If you feel that is a really big step for you, then you can opt for self-study. Have you ever thought about that too? Self-study is a type of learning process where one teaches him or herself without the help of a second person.

In order words, you will have to read and learn about Project Management all by yourself. However, this comes with lots of responsibilities that will need you to have a whole lot of time on your side. And if you are a busy man, then this is what you should do. There is Project Management certification that doesn't really require much of your time. Instead of wasting time in classes or reading large books, all you need to do is take limited classes and sit for the exam afterward. Be that as it may, it is important to know that all these can only give you the necessary certification, experience, and knowledge that you seek in the field of Project Management but will not make you successful automatically in it.

Thus, I will advise you not to confuse yourself in such a way. The successful and topnotch Project Managers you see or may have heard about didn't get to where they are today by just getting certified. Yes, being certified is a big step in becoming successful in this field. It gives legitimacy and competency to your reputation and skill. A lot of clients out there might not be too convinced even if you are extremely good at what you do. Someone of them might even ridicule or not take you seriously at all no matter how hard you try to influence and prove your worth. That is the power of Project Management certificate.

These topnotch Project Managers have their certificates. But aside from this, there are lots of steps that must be taken, lots of sacrifices that must be done, and lots of things that must change about you if you really want to be successful in this field. According to the recent statistics of the total population of Project Managers (both official and unofficial) in the United States of America, the population is known to have exceeded a little over 5,000. Now, imagine yourself as a beginner in the midst of these 5,000 other Project Managers out there, what a competition, yeah?

As scary as that may sound, I want you to know that being a successful Project Manager doesn't have anything to do with it. Though the rigorous competition for clients, the stiff labor market, and so much more would definitely have an impact either directly or indirectly on your chances of becoming successful in this field. Nevertheless, a lot of these factors lie solely in you. Before we begin, let me ask you an important question. Do you believe in yourself? Do you have faith in yourself? Do you make the decision to be a Project Manager because you want to or because you just felt like it? Is Project Management what you really crave for?

If you can answer these questions correctly and the answers are promising, then trust me, there is absolutely nothing you won't be able to accomplish in the field of Project Management. There would be no obstacle and challenge you wouldn't be able to surpass. There would be no hurdle you wouldn't be able to cross over so as to triumph and in the end become successful. Becoming successful in this field requires such determination. There are a lot of times when your relationship as a Project Manager and your client would really want to go south. At all times, you need to always work with the 3Cs in order to solve the problem – courage, confidence, and control.

In this chapter, we would look into the various steps in which one can follow in order to be a formidable force in this line of Management. We would also delve into ways in which you can be successful in Project Management. The goal of every businessman or woman, entrepreneur, and even the government is to always achieve success in every one of their endeavors. These endeavors are mostly in the form of projects. A businessman might be willing to create a new pitch or even new software for his declining business so as to change the fate of that business. The best person for the job is a Project Manager who is vast in knowledge and skill as regards that project.

In another example, if the United States of America is willing to construct a whole new building for the homeless or orphans roaming in the streets, the best way to go about it is to award the contract out to a construction company. It is this construction company that will put together a formidable team which will be headed by a Project Manager. You get my drift? These are examples of how important Project Managers are in society. Project Management is our everyday activities. It is in our everyday life. If we look at it closely, even our life is a project and we are the Project Managers. The way we handle it will determine if we are successful Project Managers or very bad Project Managers.

Whether you admit it or not, Project Management has become a very important part of every professionalism put there. From the construction industry down to information technology, textile, arts and craft, education, and so much more. It's like we can't do without keeping our activities straight and the only people that can help us in straightening them out is the Project Managers. Little wonder why the demand for them is on the rise and many people finding themselves in this position even without much experience and knowledge.

Thus, if you find yourself here out of the blue or through churns of events, then I would advise you to pay very close attention to this chapter. Here, I will be showing you how to come out of your shell and conquer the world of Project Management with your in-depth skills. I'm very sure if I ask you to define who a Project Manager is, all you will be able to tell me is that he or she manages projects. That is correct but doesn't really cover what the Project Manager does. What a Project Manager does is quite numerous and for he or she to be successful at his or her job, then he or she must have perfected these numerous duties.

Now, as a beginner, I would advise you to focus on what is real. That is the only way you can triumph over every obstacle. Additionally, you will need to be very patient as climbing the ladder to success in this field is not a day's journey. Though the journey of a thousand mile begins with one step, one has to be very bold before being able to take that bold step. If you are patient enough, continuously trying hard to better yourself, and being consistent, then becoming successful in this field shouldn't be something hard to pull off. Here are the steps to follow in becoming a successful Project Manager;

1. Be the people's person: This is the key every topnotch Project Managers out there hold dear. As a Project Manager, it is important for you to be charismatic and extremely friendly at all times. Trust me, your work would only become easier when people around you (workers and team members) love you and want to really work with you. Also, as a Project Manager, there is every possibility that your work would take you to different places where you will definitely meet different people.

   The first thing you should do is to the first relationship with the people you will be working with. Make sure you strike an understanding and get them to like you if possible. In order words, don't forget that you are only a Project Manager and not a tyrant. Don't expect all of them to follow your lead immediately. Sometimes, you would have to earn their trust first. This happens all the time. Thus, it is your duty as a Project Manager to make that happen. If you want to be successful in this field, then you need to develop your people's skills.

If your people's skills are great, then you will be able to keep and maintain your relationships with your workers and clients even better. You will also be able to freely communicate amongst one another. A good communication network is necessary for a successful project. Never forget that. Always pay very close attention to the emotions of your team members. This is also very important. If you can keep to that, then your self-confidence would definitely skyrocket.

Sometimes, the only key ingredient we might need for a project to be successful as a Project Manager is understanding our fellow teammates. When we motivate them when the need arises. When we are impartial in solving crises within. When we stay clear of cultural and religious differences amongst our team, it will only boost the respect and love our team members will have for us. That is the only way to have a good outcome. And a good outcome equates to being successful in this field.

2. Communication is key: As a Project Manager, when you communicate with your team members, then it should definitely be punchy, direct, and full of reasons. Trust me, the way we talk presents us to our fellow workers. If you are the talkative type, then I will advise you to always caution yourself so as not to lose the respect and control of your team. Learn to communicate and address your team like a professional. There should be time for everything.

There should be time for jokes and time to be serious. Always make that certain in your project team. Additionally, always stress the importance of communication amongst yourselves. Trust me, when you do that, it would relax the tempo and mood of your team. They would find it easy to say what is on their mind, be it an idea or a complaint. In cases of task sharing, always be audible and clear enough. Make sure you communicate clearly so as not to cause any further complications.

Communicate with your clients often too. That way, you will be able to know where and how to help out. Communicate with the contractors, with the customers, with the vendors, and even with the stakeholders. When you have a good rapport with these people, you will be able to carry everyone along and at the same time paving way for your career to be more successful.

3. Pay close attention to the weaknesses and strengths of your team: A good Project Manager is like a Psychologist, they always make sure they read the people around them as well as their environment so as to know how to better serve or relate with them. Do you want to be successful in this field? Then how about becoming a Psychologist? Always pay close attention to the strength and weakness of your team. Know each person's limit so as not to overload them with tasks and functions.

If you are familiar with everyone's strength and weaknesses, you will be able to relate with them better. That way, your working relationship will definitely improve and the project will become successful in no time. Additionally, knowing the strength and weakness of a team puts you at the forefront of the whole project. That way you will be able to make accurate predictions and even use that opportunity to unlock the potentials in your team.

In order to be successful as a Project Manager, it is important to know your whole team like the back of your hand. That way, you will be able to know which team member would be able to drive your project to success. You will be able to know which team member will slack off and probably pull you back. Additionally, you will be able to know when and how to share these tasks amongst your team.

4. Gain experiences or more knowledge during the course of your numerous projects: As a professional, there is always an opportunity for you to always upgrade and improve yourself by gaining more experience by the day. In Project Management, there is always an avenue where the Project Managers are liable to further their education either through direct learning or an online session and build their portfolio as well as working on numerous projects (either volunteer or freelance).

But whichever you decide, always know that the choice is entirely yours and both are good for your Project Management career. If you choose to further your studies in Project Management, then it's all good. But if you are focused on building your experience in this field, then I will suggest you start with small projects. As a beginner, that is the only way you can move forward and become an expert. Little by little, you can then move into larger jobs and projects. You will be shocked at how much you have developed and improved after a short while.

5. Always remember that you are just a Project Manager and not a tyrant: Many people that had failed in this line of Management always fall into this trap. According to some of them, being at the top of the food chain gives one so much joy and happiness that it often get into one's head. It takes discipline and a selfless person not to misuse the power. This is why you should always put it at the back of your mind that you are just a Project Manager and the project is what connects you to your client and team members.

Don't just give orders, learn to carry everyone along. Many Project Managers end up making this mistake. Don't be one of them. You alone can never know it all. That is why you have other team members in the first place. Always carry them along. Give them a listening ear. You will be shocked at the new and exciting idea they will bring forth. That way, your work will even become much easier. But when you shut your teammates up or even neglects their views, they may end up ganging up against you.

There is nothing wrong in stooping low for

your teammates, especially if they have a brilliant idea. Also, there is nothing wrong with giving them the floor when they have something to share. This will never take away your leadership neither will it reduce your position. Always strive to be the Project Manager that keeps everyone happy and excited about working. Trust me, when your team is happy, the project will definitely take good shape.

6. Always believe in yourself and your team: The beginning of every failure is when you lose hope, trust, and belief in yourself and in the people surrounding you. No matter what, always keep the faith. Even if things aren't going so well, never lose hope in your team. Always find a way to motivate them until the very end. This is the work of a leader. There is a difference between setting expectations for your team and when your team also set expectations for you. Always know the difference and balance these two.

Try to get close to your team members. Know them to a great extent. Spend time with them. If you want, you can even spend time outside working hours with them. At least, that will allow you to know them to an extent. That way, you will be able to know their plans and ideas. If you end up knowing this, then you can perfect it together. Afterward, trust in it no matter what. This will even give them enough confidence and boost their morale even more. Believing in them is what they need in order to overwork themselves gladly if the need arises.

Being a Project Manager is easy, but being the best amongst the rest is not a day's job. It's something that must be achieved by making sure every department agrees to your directives and control. All Project Managers want to be successful. Just like all beginners wants to move up the food chain. You alone can be the Project Manager you want to be. All you need to do is just to believe in yourself and lines will fall in pleasant places for you.

Chapter Six

Common Mistakes you would Encounter as a Beginner

As a beginner, you should always have it at the back of your mind that mistakes would surely happen. Whether you plan for it or not, you will definitely make them and sometimes, in more than one way. Now, when this happens, do not work yourself up or even beat yourself about it. Mistakes only signify confidence and perfection. When we make mistakes, then it shows we are beginning to get the concept of whatever we are learning. Also, mistakes are a reminder that would remind us of how much we have developed or improved.

Even the so-called experts and topnotch Project Managers out there had also made lots of mistakes at a certain point in their life. For example, being obnoxious to the whole team can cause failure and that is a mistake you don't want to make. Some also make the mistake of being a tyrant instead of a team player. They often forget that the Project Manager position is almost the same as that of a team member. Thus, making it look as if they are invincible. These and more are the common mistakes many people make in today's world.

Sometimes, we can't even see the truth in front of us when we are so carried away by these mistakes. It's like a blindfold that veils our very own eyes. It is only after we had committed and made the mistake, then our eyes will begin to see the reality of thing for what they truly are. Additionally, mistakes do happen. You don't expect to have a mistake-free journey into the world of Project Management as a beginner, do you? Especially with the amount of stiff competition out there in the market, you are bound to make a mistake or two along the way.

Now, making these mistakes is not matter but bouncing back from it and rising from your fall is what should hold substance. This is how successful people in this field are made. This is how they are built. Those topnotch Project Managers you envy today have also had their own share of mistakes and downfall, but they never let it weigh them down. As a go-getter, they were always poised with the mindset of going forward no matter what. Let this be your watchword and mantra, you will be shocked at how much you will progress within the shortest time.

This chapter would highlight some of the numerous mistakes common with beginners like you in this field. It would make you feel normal about it and even suggest probable ways to stop yourself from making such mistakes. As a beginner, many people out there that had just stumble upon or find themselves in this part of the professional world often get bullied easily by the big guns in the game, thereby, making them lose balance and focus easily. That way, they would easily make mistakes due to their lack of self-confidence and control.

According to Damian, he once stressed the fact that a lot of all these experienced Project Managers once tried to bully him into submission when he was still a beginner. He stated that he was once a team member when he started out his Project Management career and was very good at it with fresh ideas running through his mind every now and then. On an occasion where things weren't going the right way and the whole project was in jeopardy, he had the right ideas that would put the project back on time in no time. However, his Project Manager was a stumbling block. Now, what did Damian do? Your guess is as good as mine. He took the bull by the horn.

According to him, he marched straight to the client office one Tuesday morning and poured out his well-detailed idea which was welcomed by the client. The client was impressed not just by his brilliance but by his level of confidence and control. These are the key ingredients you need to possess in order to excel in this line of profession. Now, if you look at this case closely, you would realize that there are lots of mistakes and loopholes surrounding it. Also, there are lots of lessons to be learned from it as a beginner in this field of Project Management.

First, the Project Manager made a mistake of not being friendly and accommodating with his or her team members. Always know that they are your family and not your slaves. Treat them right and respect their feelings & emotions. Secondly, as a beginner, don't make the mistake of allowing a superior break you into submission, especially if you are on the right track. Always exude confidence and do the needful if the need arises. Many beginners are bound to be scared and will most likely keep mute even if the solution to save the day lies in their hand. Always be outspoken, especially when you are making sense. Be like Damian and you will achieve success in no time.

Don't be scared to take action as a Project Manager. If at all you are making a mistake, they always listen to the voice of reason. Always listen to the ideas of your team members. Mistakes have no master. No matter your level of certificates and the amount of experience you have gathered over the years, we are still liable to make mistakes. Meanwhile, when all these happen, be fast about getting them back on track. Delay can be very dangerous. No one wants a bad review on their reputation. Mistakes lead to mismanagement and mismanagement leads to failure.

Additionally, all projects can never be the same. Even if they are the same, the people, the clients, the behavior, the skills around you, the directives, and so much more surrounding the project will never be the same no matter how hard we turn it. Thus, you should stop treating every project in the same way. Make sure you understand and know how to handle each project and the team they come with. Most times, you won't have the luxury of selecting your own team. You might just be appointed to head a team of strangers. When that happens, then how would you go about it? Handling projects the same way would certainly put your projects in jeopardy. Now, here are the common mistakes a beginner in the field of Project Management would certainly encounter;

1. Incorrect scheduling: This can derail and jeopardize a project in no time. When you miscalculate the schedule of the project wrongly, you are only extending the time frame, thereby causing unnecessary and wasteful spending of scarce resources. That way, the costs of the project would certainly skyrocket and that is bad for business. The client would not only go crazy about this mismanagement but also relieve you of your position if you aren't lucky.

    Thus, always get your planning and scheduling right. Don't resist the help of others. Remember, your team is there for a reason. Let them help you. As a beginner, you might not be able to get the correct schedules of the whole project. Don't beat yourself about it. This kind of mistake happens all the time. But the ability to realize this mistake and correct them is what matters.

2. Taking decisions and actions independently: This is very common with beginners and experts in the field of Project Management. When the whole team realizes their roles and responsibilities, then things will fall into place. The team is there for a reason and that is to help you make the right decisions. Thus, always ensure that you reach a consensus with your team before taking action.

Always make sure you take them along with every one of your decisions and actions. Desist from taking decisions without proper consultations with your team. There are certain things your team members may add or subtract from your deduction. They may even add a useful idea that will benefit the whole project. In the same vein, I will recommend you always hold a general meeting with your team before taking action.

That way, you will be able to know their views. This will also make them accord a great level of respect to you in the end. When you involve them in the decision-making process, it will further improve the relationship between yourself and your team members. Additionally, there would be a sense of accountability, ownership, and dependence in the team. And this is a very good sign of success.

3. Always dismantle or dissolve complex projects into smaller bits: Always make sure you engage yourself in this particular act as it would only lead to a more successful project outcome. Are you finding it difficult to plan and execute a project? Do you feel stressed out as the project just seems more complex by the day? Then how about breaking it into pieces? How about managing it in bits instead of the complicated whole? This is one mistake beginners make.

No matter how they try managing a project, it just gets out of hand. Now, instead of them to break this project into bits, they will be trying hard to find a way through. This unsuccessful trial can be time wasting and extremely stressful. Aside from the energy and time, one will waste, one will also waste resources, and many other important things that will make the project a success. Thus, breaking the project into bits seems like the best thing to do.

Trust me, it will be more comfortable to handle and manage. You will now be able to confidently solve every problem facing the project so as to reach the desired outcome. That way, even the impossible can be possible. Now how do you go about this? It's simple. As a beginner, you just can start breaking up projects into bits without the necessary checks and balances. First, you need to understand the project. Make sure you immerse yourself to it and study it closely before breaking it into smaller pieces.

4. Not keeping your priorities straight: Always know what your priorities are and make sure you separate them from the rest. There are lots of cases where many Project Managers out there give priority to the wrong and irrelevant projects, thereby, losing out in the important ones. If you fall into this category, then you really need to start getting it right this time around. If the project you are handling is just too much, then prioritizing them is of utmost importance.

Always communicate the importance of every project to your team members. That way, they will be able to prepare adequately for the project no matter the level of priority. Many projects end up failing because of the low amount of seriousness placed on it. When conditions that matter or things that should be held in high esteem are being held merely, then the project is bound to fail.

5. Not being the people's person: Project Management entails the combination of different segments into a whole. It involves the coming together of more than one person into achieving the desired result. Now, as a Project Manager, don't make the mistake of not being the people's person. The job is not only about managing costs, benefits, schedules, plans, budgets, and so much more but to also manage the people around you. Your relationship with your team would showcase the kind of Project Manager you are.

Thus, keep your team close. Establish a good relationship with them. Always let them know that their efforts are being appreciated. If there is a good working relationship in the team, then success wouldn't be farfetched. But if the team's relationship is not something to write home about, the project is going to drag on for long and eventually fails in the end. There will be wasteful events. Now, how do you grow your relationships with your team?

Always be the understanding boss. Make sure you are familiar with your team's weaknesses and strength. Additionally, be aware of their emotions. That way, you will be able to tell the exact amount of work each person would be able to handle. It shouldn't be all about work. How about taking time to celebrate with the team outside working hours? That is one of the easiest ways of bonding.

6. Always doing things your own way: Your team is there for a reason and that is to help you take the project to the next level. Instead of letting them out most of the time, why not include them in every of your decision. Cultivate the habit of communicating wife them when the need arises. And when you communicate, make sure you are professional about it. Always be clear and punchy. That way, there would be no mix-up. For example, if you are sharing roles and responsibilities, then always be audible and clear.

Communication is key to every successful project. You should make sure there is a good communication network between you and the team, stakeholders, client, customers, and so much more. This would definitely aid your work even faster. And always make sure you organize a meeting to aid the communication process. Some of your team members might not be much of a talker, so this meeting should be an avenue for them to share their ideas.

7. Avoiding the use of Project Management tool:

The tools are there for a reason, why aren't you using them? They will not only equip you with amazing features that will help you move your project to the next level but also create a stress-free process for you all through the project. The Project Management tools are there to make your project meet its deadline. This would also make you pinpoint vital boosters which can be used in making sure your project stays afloat no matter the pressure either from within or outside.

8. Adjust if you have to, and be fast about it: Whenever you feel things aren't adding up, then do the needful. Sometimes, most beginners out there just end up sticking to a particular strategy, method, technique, tool, and other enhancements for no reason at all. For you to be extremely successful in this field, then you have to be very dynamic in your ways. You have to possess the ability to adapt and adjust to the situation on the ground no matter how shrewd it may be. And when you adapt, make sure it's fast, so as not to end up being too late.

Thus, when things start going south, don't just stick to one particular method. Try to tweak them altogether. Don't be scared of failing. I know you might be wondering what would happen if you fail the project. Thus, the reason for being reluctant in trying out new ways and sticking to your traditional ways. Well, all successful Project Managers had also taken a risk at a point in their lives, thus, don't be scared of doing the same.

Additionally, always keep everyone abreast with the situation of things no matter how bad they might end up getting. This would help you set things straight. It will also help create more time for you and your team in adjusting and coming up with solutions to any problem you are facing. Don't be scared to tweak the budget, the schedule, the cost, the benefit, and so much more so long it would help put your project in a good perspective.

Mistakes can happen to anybody no matter how skilled or knowledgeable you might be. What matters is how fast you can turn the mistake into your strength. Now ask yourself how fast can you make your mistakes your strength? Sometimes, all we need is just a single mistake before we can actually summon up the courage to reach greater heights. Be the Project Manager that always wants more. The next chapter promises to be amazing and quite interesting, you don't want to miss it.

Chapter Seven

New Trends in Project Management

Do you know that there are lots of new and exciting trends that had taken over Project Management? Why go through the traditional process of doing things in this line of professionalism when there are new improved versions and ways in which you can make things happen. Project Management is an exciting field where things change every day. What you know as the most sophisticated and easily applicable tool this year might be obsolete the next year to come. That is how things work in this line of professionalism.

Thus, if you really want to make things work for you as a beginner, if you want to always have control over any project you handle, and if you want to be successful in no time, then you need to stay abreast with the recent trend in this field. One mistake beginners make is to stay glued to a particular technique or method in getting things done in Project Management. This is why I will strongly recommend you always go with the flow each time. Always be familiar with every new trend out there. Make sure you follow the world in every direction they will face.

Additionally, the struggle towards taking Project Management to the next level is very real. Project Managers no longer want to stay stagnant and traditional anymore, thus, leading to the development of more advanced tools, techniques, and methods that had taken over the field completely. In the same vein, I will suggest that you join the ride towards this new and exciting adventure. As Project Management evolves with new trends, it is pertinent for you to also meet up.

For example, instead of racking up your head and brain in planning a project manually, there are lots of new ways on which that function can be executed neatly, easily, and fast. Even though you don't have the necessary power and might to exude these new trends, you can still stick to the old means. But, not without making sure you stay updated always about the ongoing trends. That way, you won't feel left out in the excitement and development. No one will have the confidence to call you an archaic Project Manager.

As a beginner, I will advise you to cut your coat according to your size. Not every beginner out there has the privilege of having the power and means to these new trends. Thus, starting traditional won't be a bad idea. You can plan, execute, and make your project successful by following the traditional means. But with time, you should be able to upgrade your methods, tools, and techniques gradually into new and trending ones. This would even make you become better and familiar with both old and new trends.

Like we all know, Project Management cut across all corners and areas of professionalism. From areas of construction down to manufacturing, textile, education, health, finance, transportation, and so much more. Thus, the need for Project Managers in the world today. If Project Managers are in high need in the society today, would it be at your own advantage if you stay afloat in the tides of Project Management? Wouldn't it be at your own advantage if you become familiar and finally employ sophisticated and new trends into your way of planning and executing projects?

A construction Project Manager would definitely treat a project differently from the way a Finance Project manager would treat a project. An Information Technology Project Manager would treat a project differently from the way a Transportation Project Manager would also treat a project. Thus, it is very important to know that these diverse Project Managers vary in their methods and techniques. But still, it doesn't stop them from employing the same new trend in their business.

For you to be a successful Project Manager and for you to move from a beginner stage to an expert one in no time, then you must stay glued to these trends. This chapter would enlighten you on the various trends that had taken over the world of Project Management. Also, it would show you how to use these trends to your own advantage even as a beginner. Like I explained earlier, these trends are changing rapidly. They are not stagnant like its traditional counterpart, thus, there is a need for you to always stay updated.

The year 2019 had been great so far as regards Project Management. There had been lots of exquisite trends that had been introduced in the field of Project Management. So what are these trends? Here they are;

1. AI (Artificial Intelligence): The world has changed a lot in terms of technology. Thanks to new innovations and development, Artificial Intelligence has come to stay. It won't be farfetched from the truth if we say that AI is the latest trend in every aspect of the world. In every sector and industry, this new trend had found its footing and at the same time become the driving force behind every success. It is the talk of the town.

    There are lots of applications which would make your work very easy. For example, Siri on Apple and Samsung devices. This app is a talking AI which would help you put things in order. You will be shocked at how fast Siri would help you organize your project. It would help you collate the figures properly. Google is also a search engine that would make your work faster. In case you are stuck or making no headway, you can easily check Google and find out how many people had solved the problem you are having.

That way, your productivity, and output will definitely triple. AI will give you a platform where you will be able to connect even better with your team members, client, stakeholders, and so much more. With lots of amazing applications to choose from, you will be able to move your Project Management skills to the next level. Your work will be more efficient and effective. You will be surprised at how these amazing applications will give you vital suggestions, correct your mistakes, and arrange your work neatly.

2. Hybrid Approach: It is important to know that the traditional method that seeks to use the same process and procedure doesn't really hold value any longer. It is pertinent to know that this one-size-fits-all-strategy no longer hold the same power as it had in the past century. In recent time, there are lots of approaches that are now trending and taken the place of this traditional approach.

Additionally, you can also interchange both traditional and modern approach to suit your project. It all depends on the kind of project you are handling. This is what is known as the Hybrid Approach. A lot of Project Managers out there don't just rely on one particular type of approach. Like we said earlier, what makes a successful Project Manager is the ability to tweak these approaches. When the project seems to be more complex and extremely large, then I will recommend you to make use of the hybrid approach.

Project Management today has taken a whole new dimension. Projects are no longer as easy as they used to be. They are now shrewd, complex, and tougher. Thus, the need for a switch between the traditional and modern approach – Hybrid Approach. Be that as it may, I will advise you to be a hybrid Project Manager. That way, you will be able to handle any project that comes your way with any problem.

3. Emotional Intelligence (EQ): Emotional Intelligence is a new trend in the world of professionalism. Many people don't pay much attention to Emotional Intelligence but trust me, this is one trend that has taken over the world by storm. A lot of companies out there has now given Emotional Intelligence a lot of recognition and cognizance. There is a possibility that we might get lost in the advanced methodologies and

techniques as a beginner, thus, the need for being Emotionally Intelligent.

Additionally, Emotional Intelligence would give us a much-needed advantage over others. By understanding other people, we will be able to know how to relate with them as well as influence the decisions of our team members and clients. Emotional Intelligence is a very useful weapon that we can use to reach a greater height in the field of Project Management. Emotional Intelligence will build you up emotionally and your relationship with people would improve rapidly.

This would ensure your career follow a straight path. If your team is filled with people of different cultural, ethnic, and religious background, Emotional Intelligence would help you manage them perfectly. It would help you understand every individual irrespective of their background. You will be able to resolve conflicts in the team. You will be able to understand your team's emotions. Trust me, Emotional Intelligence is the new trend.

4. PMO (Project Management Office): In recent times, the PMO had been gaining momentum due to their outstanding and amazing performance over the last few years. It might interest you to

know that the PMO holds the key to the success of your project. In order words, you cannot have a successful project without paying extra attention to the PMO. In case you are wondering why the PMO is so important or becoming increasingly popular by the day, then here is why.

The PMO is the bridge between project failure and its success. It is the stimulant that ensures all projects get to their desired destination and that is being successful. It is what pushes the project into attaining its goals and objectives without many hurdles along the way. The PMO stands between the client's decision and the Project Manager's execution. I believe you can now see why you need to really hold the PMO dear to your heart as a Project Manager.

Be that as it may, recent research has it that about 42% of the total projects executed in the United States of America were only able to meet their target, goals, and objectives. And this is because they have an indomitable PMO behind them. This fact gives much cognizance and importance to the recent trend of the PMO. It shows they are the driving force of every organization and would make the project easier for you if only you can learn to acknowledge them.

5. Kanban Boards: Have you ever heard of this particular trend? If you haven't, then don't beat yourself about it. Remember you are still a beginner in the field. Besides, not all Project Management experts in the country can fully beat their chest with the knowledge of this concept. Be that as it may, Kanban is not an English word. It is, in fact, an Asian (Japanese) word meaning "Billboard". The story behind Kanban is a very funny story. Initially, it was an idea introduced by the Toyota organization in Japan to take their manufacturing process to the next level but had now found its way into the realm of Project Management.

What is Kanban? Kanban is an approach which entails the use of different Kanban cards which are spread out on a large visual board for the purpose of managing workflow and the manufacturing process. In order words, it is a way of making sure the manufacturing process are well accounted for and in the process leads to a more improved way of managing the affairs of the organization. For Project Managers, Kanban would serve as a new way of finding new ways towards managing the project.

Instead of sticking to the old methods, Kanban would serve as a whole new method one can make use of. It would also open the minds of

Project Managers into seeing things differently. Kanban is indeed a sophisticated innovation. When your projects are flexible and change frequently in time, schedule, and so much more, then this Kanban approach is the best approach to employ. Today, Kanban is a force to reckon with in the world of Project Management. It would allow you to hold control of the project and push stagnation further away.

6. Analytics: Most times Project Management is all about crunching those numbers. Thus, what better way can one go about it other than Analytics? Analytics is a better method of calculating and dealing with numbers. Instead of going about it the old and traditional way, Analytics will provide you with a more sophisticated way. In addition, it's going to make calculations easy and less stressful. What you would normally spend hours racking your brain on would now be solved at very little time.

Analytics would give you more time to look into the details of your results. That way, you would be able to easily sieve out what is wrong from what is right. Aside from the calculations, you can also check out the performance of the team so far. One advantage of Analytics is the ability to present you with raw facts and data.

These are many more are the reasons why it is trending in today's world.

7. Cybersecurity: It is important to know that the internet comes with its advantages and disadvantages, with its blessings and its curses, and with its strength and weaknesses. No matter how little and insignificant your data might be, you never can tell who is snooping around. If you are a beginner in this field, then you should know that cybersecurity is an important trend which must be taken seriously so as not to lose your data to cybercriminals.

You should know that there is a need for you to always have at least one potent firewall installed in your devices. This would help sieve out hackers that are willing to steal your data. Always secure your plans else they will end up getting compromised with you even having the slightest idea. Every Project Manager has his or her own secret strategy, plan or method that works magic for him or her. Unless you are willing to share this secret weapon of yours, then I will suggest you keep it safe no matter what.

Don't be left behind. Don't be outdated and archaic. Be the modern Project Manager by making yourself stay abreast with different new trends that have taken over the world as a whole.

Sometimes, clients like seeing that their Project Managers are sophisticated and modern. This would keep their mind at peace. Keep yourself updated and join the winning team.

Chapter Eight

Project Planning

As a Project Manager, this is, in fact, one of your main jobs in the field or outside the field. The term Project Management alone depicts serious planning, thus, making the Project Manager the best planners amongst planners. We all get to know a good Project Manager from the way he or she manages the team and plan his or her events. Additionally, the success of the project lies solely with the planning skills of the Project Manager and his whole team.

Imagine being a beginner in the field of Project Management and you don't even know how to plan a project effectively and efficiently, what does that make you? You will instantly lose the support of the team as well as that of the people around you. Aside from planning for a project, how about planning our lives appropriately? First, we are an individual before becoming a Project Manager, thus, the need to plan our lives. If our personal affairs are in order, then it's going to reflect well on our professional life.

I'd seen lots of cases where people fail to plan their personal lives well. They would give little cognizance and importance to their lives and end up messing up in their place of work. Our personal lives matter. A lot of people would come to work every day with a sorrowful heart. Sometimes with a very dull mood, thereby, affecting everybody they come in contact with at work. Don't think because you are a Project Manager, thus, that makes you immune to such things. This assumption is very wrong.

As a Project Manager, it would only get worse, trust me. When you lose control of your life, then everything would certainly fall apart in no time. Clients would start to doubt your abilities. Your team members would start to revolt. The projects would not take good shape. Now, that is a bad thing. According to Damian. He mentioned that he had once faced this adversity in his life once or twice and it really weighed him down. His personal life was a mess and it really made him lose control and focus. Planning a project effectively became very difficult.

He mentioned a small tiff with his wife which escalated into a bigger one just because he was a good planner as a Project Manager but didn't know he was a very bad one at home. It took him a lot to realize this fact that was staring deep into his eyes. And when he did, he made sure he never made such mistake ever again. That is the power Planning wields. Now, if this can happen to anyone when making awful plans in your personal life, what do you think would happen to you if you really suck at Project Planning?

I will strongly recommend you become read extensively about this topic. It is one of the most outstanding attributes in a Project Manager Clients would always notice first. In order to move from this beginner stage to an expert one, then you need to up your Project Planning game. Now, what would this chapter do? This chapter would familiarize you with what real Project Planning is without sugarcoating its true meaning. It would immerse you with the fact that Planning is very important as a Project Manager and as an individual. And all these would be alongside the processes and steps to follow in order to plan a good Project.

Be that as it may, you will be shocked to know that Project Planning is more than just sitting down alone in your office while scribbling down diagrams and codes best known to you. It is more than that. It is, in fact, an aspect of team bonding. It is a way of connecting with your team. It is a way of proving the point that "many good heads are actually better than one". This is what planning means. It is a means of drawing up points, ideas, and will in order to execute an action. That is what planning means. Remember, you can't do this alone. Your team is there for a reason, always carry them along. And if you feel you must do this alone or had already perfected a plan before the arrival of your team then feel free to share your amazing plan with them. You will be shocked at how helpful their feedbacks would be.

Just imagine this scenario as a beginner in the field of Project Management. After a careful perusal of your credentials and resume, even after knowing that you are still a newbie in this line of professionalism, the client still decides to take a chance on you. I'm sure you would want to impress his or her that choosing you was a wise decision. Now that you've gotten the job, what do you plan on doing first? Sharing your plans becomes the next best thing to do, yeah?

You would want to blow their minds away with an amazing performance and presentation. In this line of professionalism, the first impression matters a lot. So, let's say you have every necessary tool, technique, the methodology at your disposal, how then do you go about making the best out of them? How do you go about making a very good Project Plan? If your project is quite difficult for you to handle, then breaking it into bits in order to effectively manage it becomes the only solution. However, if it is relatively easy at the same time, then lucky you.

Now, how do you go about your project plan? Remember your client and stakeholders would want to see an impressive presentation, how would you go about it? After making you the Project Manager, they must have kept you abreast the situation of the organization. They must have familiarized you with their hopes and aspirations. They must have shown you what they are expecting from you and their hope is for you to deliver. All these might seem crazy at first. As a beginner, it might seem very hard to comprehend. Trust me, I've also been there.

Especially when you start seeing terms and concepts you've never come across before. Now, this is where you need to get your act together. This is where you need to be focused and remember, do not panic no matter the pressure or complications. Even if the time frame is short, always be confident of yourself. Know how to utilize every tool you've got. Your team is a helping hand, use it well too. There are things they know and you don't, don't be too proud to ask if you don't know. We all don't know everything.

Now, how do we plan a project? Where do we go from here? How do we go about it? What steps do we follow to come out with a good plan? It's pretty simple. This chapter would enlighten you on the six basic steps one can follow is coming up with an amazing plan which would blow the minds of your client and stakeholders away. Here they are;

1. Understand what your clients, customers, and stakeholders want: This is the first step towards reaching the goals and aspirations of your clients, customers, and stakeholders. You can't plan a project without knowing and understanding what

they want. Remember, the project you are about to plan belongs to them in the first place. Thus, make sure you truly understand where they are coming from. That way, both parties would remain happy at the end of the day.

Don't assume for anybody. If you know you are not clear on a particular goal, go back and ask. Make sure you are clear about what they really want. In the end, they are the ones that will be affected by the end result. Additionally, as a beginner, it would be great if you can jot down these goals from your clients. Make sure you scribble every little detail down. These should be the guiding principles that would guide you through your project.

Immerse yourself with the kind of expectations they would like to see. Use this information to create your project cost, scope, budget, scheduling, and time frame. When you do this, make sure you follow the right channel, thus, making everyone stay on the same page. This would reduce the risk of miscommunication. Also, you can be creative. Instead of settling for what your clients want, you can also tweak some of these goals and make it look more appealing and enticing. This would boost your Project Management profile.

2. 2. Make sure you prioritize the goals: This is very important so as not to waste more time, especially if the time frame is very short. Always make sure you set a scale of preference for the goals. Sometimes, your clients don't always know what they want. You might be faced with a little challenge of your client listing uncountable goals. And you and I know that all these uncountable goals can't fit into one plan. Thus, the need for prioritizing.

After understanding the goal and objectives of your clients, customers, and stakeholders, then I will suggest you sieve the best out of the rest. I will recommend you set your priorities straight, thereby, making sure your work remains as easy as it can get. Now, it is important to know that these sieved goals must reflect your client's wants and views. If they don't, then you need to start all over again. Make sure they are very clear and easily understood. This would give your team members easy access to the goal, thereby, making the project easy altogether.

3. Take the time frame seriously: There is no better way of tasking yourself into being productive other than making sure you follow the deadline.

When we put the deadlines at the back of our minds, we would be shocked at how effective and efficient our work would be. Ensure you know how to go about it also. Make sure you always know what the deliverables are. You should draw out the amount of time yourself and your team would invest every day into the project.

If you are far behind, then you should know how much time you would invest in the project. Some Project Managers end up not going home all through the night. They sometimes spend more time in the office than at home. It depends on how difficult the project is and how short the time frame is. Setting the time frame to your taste would enable you to know what your progress is from time to time. In order words, you will be able to check how far you have gone.

4. Come up with the right schedule: Scheduling is very important in Project Planning. One mistake from miscalculations and misguided schedules, then everything about your project is going to take another form. From the costs, down to the timing, the benefits, the scope, the budget, and so much more. Scheduling allows us to determine the right proportion of time, costs, and so much more to be given to a task. This would also tell you which of your team member would be responsible for the task.

Create a Gantt Chart for your scheduling process if possible. This would only allow you to locate and infuse your dependencies with the task. The Gantt chart is a mechanism that makes scheduling easy. Always make good use of it. Don't forget to share these tasks amongst your team. Remember, each member of your team has an area in which they specialize in. Give the members tasks that are best known to them so as to achieve the best results in the end.

They alone know how to handle the tasks effectively and efficiently. Your job is to make sure each of them comes with a good result afterward. Manage this congregation of brains well. Make sure they are always in line with whatever plans you've made so far. That is the only way you will be able to draw out an amazing plan at the end of the day.

5. Know the challenges and risks you are facing: The only way you can cross over a hurdle us to identify and know what it is. This is the only way you will know which type of solution to proffer. It is important to know that all projects will definitely hit rock-bottom. This can be either at the beginning, in the middle of it or even towards the end. As a beginner, I will advise you to keep this in mind so as to be readily prepared for what is coming.

Trust me, the risks will come. And when they do, always make sure you have them contained. That way, they won't pose a threat to your plans. Don't just sit there hoping for a miracle when they come knocking. You need to take the necessary steps into making sure they don't escalate into something bigger. You work as a Project Manager is not only about managing projects, it is also about managing conflicts, challenges, and at the same time risks.

You need to make sure you had foreseen any challenges or risks you might face along the line before starting out your planning process. For example, if you are working with a group of culturally, religiously, and racially different individuals, then you need to put it at the back of your mind that there is bound to be a religious, cultural or even racial conflict along the line. Thus, you would know how to effectively manage the team.

Additionally, you can always make sure your projects stay risk-free by conducting a risk assessment. Also, you can develop your own strategy for managing the risks surrounding your project planning process. That way, your project plan would be free (at least if not totally) from emerging risks.

6. Always share your break-through and update to your clients and stakeholders: This is the problem some client face with lots of Project Managers out there. When they have assigned a project to a Project Manager with a specific deadline, they no longer see that Project Manager again till the day of the presentation. This act is not really advisable, especially as a beginner. Always make sure you send updates to your client. If possible, meet them in person. They might have a new goal or angle they would want you to focus on.

Additionally, always make sure you keep your client abreast with the progress of your work. If you feel you don't want them to know what you are planning before the deadline, then you might really need to stand on your feet in order to make that happen. Some Client might prove very difficult, trust me. They would not want to make it easy on you and sometimes want to exert their authority on you. The best way to stop that from happening is to tell them beforehand. Let them know how you operate and how you like doing your thing.

And when you are making your presentations, remember first impression matters. Make sure your presentation is clear and can be easily understood by all. You can throw in a few Project Management terms to sound official and professional but don't go overboard. What is the need of going all grammatical without passing a message? Break down every complex term in order to pass your message. Trust me, communication is key when making a presentation that would blow the minds of your audience.

Planning a project is quite simple but yet complex. With the right combination of resources, putting a plan together shouldn't be added to pull off. But what if these resources are limited? How are you going to pull it off? As a Project Manager, you are expected to be versatile and this involves working under unfavorable conditions. The Project plan is vital in the success of a project, thus, make sure you pour your attention into it. The next chapter would focus on Project Control. Please flip over.

Chapter Nine

Project Control

This is a very important concept in the field of Project Management. As crazy as this may sound, a project can only be successful if the Project Manager holds enough control. Do you expect a good result from a mismanaged team? Do you expect something good out of a disorganized team? The answer is no. This is why having control of your team is very important. I want you to keep it at the back of your mind that it's not going to be easy having control of your team as a beginner. With just a little experience, many of your team members would not really want to give you their support at first.

Especially if some of them are more experienced than you. There is always going to be a need for them to act strange and most times see you as inferior. Now, when this happens, there is always a need for you to prove yourself to them. There is always a need for you to earn their trust. There is no need for violence neither is there any need for unnecessary tiffs. All you need to do is to reaffirm your position by showing them you are a part of a whole. You need to show them they are equally important and that together you will make the project a success.

Having control of a project as a Project Manager is paramount. Remember, you are in charge of managing the affairs and running of the whole team. Thus, you need to always be in charge. There is no way you would make your team work together in harmony if you don't manage them with understanding and perseverance. Having control doesn't equate to having them fear you and submit to your will even when it is clearly against their better judgment. Sometimes, most Project Managers get it wrong in this aspect. They think having control means having the rest of the team at your fingertip.

This is very wrong. Having control of your team also entails having them enjoy working with you, thereby, making them submit to your will effortlessly. Having control means having the ability to influence the views, decisions, and opinion of your team, the client, and even the stakeholders. That is real control and that is what you should aspire to have. When you have that, then the rest will definitely fall into place. The trust and support from your team will automatically grow even without you giving it your best shot. Be that as it may, not every Project Manager has to go through the struggle of blending with the team.

Some are just natural leaders and possess inborn

skills and charisma to make people fall in love with them. In other words, you might also find it easy to connect with your team even without really sweating it out. When you possess these skills and qualities, it would just make your work even easy. When you get your clients, team, and stakeholders to like you as a Project Manager, then you have automatically gained controlled without even knowing it. You will be shocked at how your clients would suddenly start becoming lenient with you. Your team would start becoming receptive and amazingly sweet. That way, making your project achieve the best possible outcome.

Now, what does this chapter tend to do? This chapter would familiarize you with what Project Control really is. It would differentiate and separate compelling with influencing. That way, teaching you the difference between the two before you start confusing both. Lastly, it would tell you how to easily exert, hold, and maintain control as a Project Manager. Trust me, you don't want to find yourself in a situation where no one in your team listens or acknowledges you as the team leader. It really sucks and at the same time would make you look terrible at your job.

But when this happens, don't sweat it. Don't beat yourself about it. Instead, look for possible ways on how to turn things around. Make sure you brace yourself up as a beginner as this may be your fate with any team whatsoever. If you are struggling with control issues on your team, then I will suggest you pay close attention to this book, especially this particular chapter.

Project Control involves a whole churn of procedures and events that involves both the cooperation of the whole team and the authority of the Project Manager throughout the project. When the Project Manager has control, he or she exerts absolute influence over everything that involves the project. From the cost levels to the budget, down to the schedule, and so much more. Now, you begin to ask yourself if the Project Manager is just there to exert his hold over everyone and everything. Well, this is another way to put it. There can be no ship with two captains. The ship would definitely capsize in the end due to disagreements and headlocks. This is the same thing for a project. It will definitely fail in the end.

Thus, the need for Project Control. When you confidently oversee the tasks and levels of each part of Project, then you boldly say that you are in control. Mind you, some client can be very controlling. Remember, it is their project you are dealing with ad aside you, no one wants the best for the project aside from the. To them, the project is more than a project. It is like their child, thus, they would most times get skeptical about every turn and decision you make. Project Control is compulsory traits or skills the Project Manager must infuse in his or her Project Management experiences so as to be able to come up with amazing results.

This is not something he or she should have for the benefit of the project alone. It is something he or she must possess as a Project Manager. If you have control over your project, then there would be no problem of mismanagement. Everything would definitely play out as it was planned exactly. Be that as it may, when we mention the term Project Control, then you should know we are only referring to three important things – Setting Standards for yourself and your project, Measuring Performance all through the project, and at the same time Taking corrections when the need arises. Thus, here are the important ways to making sure you gain control of your team, your project, your client, your customers, and probably your stakeholders.

1. Make sure you always hold meetings: Having control can also mean giving listening ears to your team members. When you respect their opinion and listen to their view about a particular task, then you are in turn creating an avenue for team bonding. One of the most effective ways of doing this is to hold meetings with them regularly and efficiently. In the meetings make sure you outline and reemphasize on the need for completing the goals and objectives of the project.

    Throw in a few friendly jokes if possible. Make the atmosphere mild and conducive for all team members in any way that you can. If you show your team members that you trust and acknowledge their view, they will, in turn, give their loyalty to you in return. That way, you would be controlling them even without trying. Make sure the communication network is very effective. As a Project Manager, the only way to control your team is to manage them appropriately. This is your job. To utilize every resource towards the success of a project. Don't forget that.

Always show that you are a professional in this field, that way, they will be more submissive. Begin every meeting in a good note, just like a professional. These meetings will show you how far you had come and how far you need to go. The meetings would also showcase how much control you have on the team. Trust me, the control process can be very complicated. One minute it would look like you are great at it and the next, it would totally look frustrating. Thus, always be yourself. Share the tasks according to the skills your team members possess. Don't be bias in your dealings. Always make sure you are clear and understood.

2. Always perform quality control in your team: Additional, you might want to check the amount of hold you have on your project and how much this hold had delivered. The best way to go about

this is via Quality Control. This would show you where you need to focus more on in the project and which areas need a little slacking off. Quality control is there to make you exert your influence on the team as a Project Manager. It is a reminder to your team members that you are in charge, thus, your decision on any task is final.

In a situation where you are faced with insubordination or lack of control in your team. You can check these situations by performing quality control in the department where this insubordination is emanating from. In order words, you can use quality control as a weapon which would shut down this gross misconduct. Quality control would put more pressure on them and more grace to you. Now how do you perform Quality Control? It's simple.

Quality Control is more like a test which is carried out on a product before it finally reaches its final destination – the consumers. Be that as it may, your clients would definitely want to see the quality of the product or project you are heading. Thus, one can say this is a compulsory phase you must pass through. Nevertheless, it is a weapon you should use in order to gain the respect and control you truly need for a successful project.

3. Always measure and be updated of the progress

so far: This is one hell of a weapon that will keep your team on their toes all through the project. When you set timelines and deadlines for a particular task, it shows you possess the authority and control over your team. It also shows that your team is cooperating and that is a good thing. But in moments where you can't even tell them what to do and when to do it, then you need to follow this step.

You should cultivate the spirit of monitoring, staying updated, and measuring the extent to which your project had progressed. This would give you a certain amount of control. Additionally, it would also ensure that your team takes their jobs seriously and there would be no issue of delay. Staying updated is your job but you can also make good use of it as a way of influencing your team. If that happens, then your project would only have one outcome – success.

Additionally, if you feel a certain team member or members are acting strange and causing unnecessary trouble in the team, then feel free to reassign them to another task. Staying updated would give you the much need advantage and ideas you need in making sure you stay in control. You will be able to tell who and who is loyal, who and who are really not happy about the team's condition, and so much more.

That way, you would be able to find the right solution to the problems.

4. Always make sure you are active and responsive to changes: Trust me, a weak Project Manager can never succeed in this line of professionalism and I trust you don't want to fund yourself in that category. Thus, always take the necessary action when the need as rises. Never stay dormant as the leader of the team. This would only lead to insubordination and misconduct. As the head of a project, you should know that you are responsible for the failure and success of the project.

You should be able to know what is wrong from right and also know the appropriate decision and action to take in line with that. This would make sure everything goes in order. It would ensure that the costs, schedule, benefits, budgets, and so much more remain the same. The only constant thing in life is change, thus, the project will definitely take a new course with time. That is why you need to make sure you take the appropriate decisions and be ready when this happens.

If a team member misbehaves, then you should know what to do against that. If a team member performs a task well, you should know how to act also. Additionally, if the project takes a whole new shape (for example, the client wants to focus on a whole new goal and wants you to tweak this with the project without losing the point of the project), then you should be able to also make that happen.

5. Be a perfect judge amidst conflicts: One way you can use to gain control, support, and respect of your team is to be diplomatic in all things. Your ability to manage issues perfectly would always come in handy, trust me. Remember, you are a manager. Not just Project Management but also Human Management. You should also be an expert in Emotional Intelligence so as to be able to deal with the issues that would definitely come up later.

Additionally, as a Project Manager, you need to manage not just human relations but also the important issues surrounding your project. You would need to make sure everything goes hand in hand, else, the project would definitely fall apart. The cost should complement the time, the timing should complement the benefits, and the benefits should complement the budget. This is the job you've been appointed for. Know these issues, understand them, and come up with an amazing solution in the end.

Don't forget that you can always ask for ideas and opinions from your team members if you are short of it. Your team members are there for a reason and that is to help you out. Trust me, it won't make you smaller or lose control. Instead, it will only show that you are also a team player.

Having control is different from compelling or forcing others to do your bidding. Please don't confuse the two. What I am possibly referring to is when one possesses an influence on your team, client's, shareholders decisions and actions to an extent. This influence can come as a result of love, admiration, agreement or any other source. The difference between influence and compelling is a force. When your team starts fearing you, then you need to go back and check yourself. Ask yourself where you got it all wrong. Your team shouldn't be scared of you, instead, they should hold you in high esteem.

This is the kind of control I am talking about. Be that as it may, if you know you are having issues holding control in your team as a Project Manager, then there must be something holding that control. You need to go back and ask yourself what went wrong, then work towards correcting this flaw. Project control helps in making sure the project gets the desired result. Now, let's talk about the enhancements that would foster the project into reaching its desired destination. And when I say enhancements, I am talking about the key techniques, methodologies, and tools in Project Management. These and more are what the next chapter would delve into. Let's get to it, shall we?

Chapter Ten

Key Techniques, Methodologies, and Tools of Project Management

In Project Management, there are lots of methodologies, techniques, and tools which can be employed to spice up your project. You might be wondering why lots of topnotch Project Managers out there excel in any project they lay their hands on, well it's simple; they basically make use of these diverse enhancements in making sure their projects reach their desired destinations. Whenever they feel the project isn't making any headway, they turn to these diverse techniques, methodologies, and tools for help.

Many people have this notion of Project Management having a one-size-fits-all technique, method, or tool. This is a very wrong notion. With lots of exquisite enhancements out there that would make Project Management easy, fun, and successful, there is none of them that possess such quality. Don't get me wrong, each technique, methods, and tool are very flexible, reliable, and even dependable but none of them is universal. Each of them has a specific function and reason for their creation. Now, it is left for you to select the right one at the right time.

According to the Project Management Institute (PMI), and I quote;

"a methodology is defined as 'a system of practices, techniques, procedures, and rules used by those who work in a discipline."

These enhancements like I call them because they further help enhance Project Management in more than one way are very numerous in number. But for the sake of time and your level of comprehension, we would only mention a few from each part – Techniques, Methodologies, and Tools. Their primary aim is to help the Project Manager out in making sure they achieve success, no matter how little in their projects. Mind you, each of them has their own set of principles and rules. Thus, you alone will be able to decide which one is good for you and which is not. But it all depends on the nature of your project and what problems you are facing at that particular time.

Remember, these enhancements are there to make your work easier, thus, feel free to employ any of them when the need arises. Also, you can choose to use more than one enhancement at the same time. It all depends on the nature of the project you are dealing with. Thus, feel free to change from any when the need arises.

If these topnotch Project Managers can employ these enhancements to the success of their projects, then I would advise you to also pay close attention to it. This chapter would familiarize you with the basic techniques, methodologies, and tools you can employ on your projects. It would also go further to explain how you would make the maximum use of these enhancements. But first, we will begin with the key techniques, before going for the other two.

Key Techniques in Project Management

1. The traditional Project Management: Aside from the new trends that had ruled the world of Project Management in recent times, traditional Project Management had been a very reliable technique used and followed strictly in order to achieve remarkable results in the end. Here, you just need to perform the traditional roles of a Project Manager. You even carry your team along, share ideas, execute projects, and plan accordingly. If you are working on a less stressful project, then this is the best technique you can ever use.

2. 2. Waterfall Project Management: This is another way of using the advanced traditional technique. The waterfall Project Management is another technique that requires every team member to focus more on the common goal.

Here, there is a need for cooperation. Instead of team members working individually on tasks, they can come together and work closely. The waterfall project requires a whole lot of team members. This team cooperation often leads to team bonding and a better project result. This technique is very dependable on the Gantt chart.

3. Rational Unified Process: The rational unified process as a technique got its name from its developers. It is quite familiar and shares the same tenets with the iterative style of software development projects. If you are working on a consumer-product kind of Project where the consumers would have to give you their feedback, then this is the technique for you. Unlike the waterfall type of projects, the rational unified process focuses more on the views and opinions of the end users. It believes and works with the consumer view for better improvement.

4. PERT Project Management: After the cold war, there was a need for a new way of perfecting large scale Project Management. Thus, the result of the collaborative effort with the armed forces is what we know as the PERT Project Management today and it has been very helpful ever since. This particular technique is quite amazing for a one time project, especially in the manufacturing stage. Although there is always a

high chance of the project stretching out more than normal. Additionally, if you want to know how far you've come in a project, then this technique would come in handy.

5. Critical Path Project Management: One can say the Critical Path Project Management is easily the most populous techniques amongst Project Managers. Developed in the 1950s, the Critical Path technique focuses its strength on the time frame within different tasks and also the level of dependencies surrounding it. Instead of just checking your progress like that of the PERT technique, this particular technique focuses more on your priorities and how to ensure you don't stay stagnant. It would make sure it gives you the right measurement and estimates of a task, thereby, equipping you with whatever you need to make the task a success.

6. 6. Critical Chain Project Management: This is an improved version of the Critical Path technique. Its focus on the resizing and cut-down of the project team, budget, and so much more. It believes that if that happens, the amount of pressure on the project would also reduce, thus, leading to success in the end. Instead of speeding up the process as Critical Path suggested, you follow the estimated data and use that as a means in cutting down unnecessary things

surrounding the project. This is one of the most competitive techniques used in recent times.

Key Methodologies in Project Management

1. Agile: This is no doubt one of the most populous Project Management methodologies that had ever been developed. If you are working on a project that has a high chance of been repeated, then this is the methodology for you. With Agile, you can't do it alone. You will need the maximum cooperation of your team and that of your customers (in the form of feedbacks) in order to be able to find probable solutions to the problems surrounding your project. The Agile was first created and tested for software development use only until it was used outside that line. Ever since it had been a driving force for every type of Project Managers out there.

   As a direct improvement on the waterfall technique, this methodology gates it's tenets from the principles of Agile Manifesto. What is an Agile Manifesto? I will tell you. In 2001, a group of amazing and outstanding leaders of various industries (about 13 in number) made a declaration on unraveling legitimate and better methods for software development, thereby, ensuring these methods still follows a path where there would be iterative development, teamwork, and the necessary changes.

Agile is a very adaptive methodology which can be used in a whole lot of project type. It is important to know that Agile is popularly used by lots of Project Managers out there to drive home a rather difficult project. Agile also features a whole lot of functions which includes the use of the six main deliverables (product vision statement, product roadmap, product backlog, release plan, Sprint Backlog, and increment) in making sure the project remains unshaken. That way, it will further help develop an outstanding product in the end.

2. Scrum: This particular type of methodology has to deal with five different values which are commitment, courage, focus, openness, and respect. Just like Agile, it also aims at making projects reach their desired destinations. It is also perfect for the iterative type of projects. Scrum will make you deliver and develop amazing projects which will blow the minds of your clients away. Agile and Scrum are in fact two sides of the same coin. What differentiates them is the way and manner in which they are operated, else the functions and goals still remain the same.

Now, how do Scrum operate? It's quite easy. Scrum draws its strength by focusing on specially assigned roles in the team, certain events that may occur, and other artifacts surrounding the project. The roles are strictly divided into three – Product Owner, Development Team, and the Scrum Master. Scrum events are specially designed events that would make your goal become more achievable. They are the Sprint, Sprint Planning, Daily Sprint, Sprint Review, and the Sprint Retrospective,

The Scrum artifacts are in the form of logs which contains all the important list of priorities and sometimes irrelevances. This is to be double sure and not to give a chance to further problems. The Scrum artifacts include the Product Backlog and the Sprint Backlog. The former is held by the Product Owner. As a representative of the client or stakeholders, he or she has every right to hold this list. It includes everything about the project – costs, benefits, budgets, functions, and so much more. The Sprint Backlog contains the necessary information for the execution of the next sprint.

3. Kanban: We have already made references to this in one of our earliest chapters. Believe it or not, Kanban is making waves and is a methodology that is trending in today's world. Just like Scrum,

it also has the same tenets with Agile. Initially, Kanban was a brainchild of the Toyota production organizations during the 1940s and had ever since found its way into the world of Project Management. How did this happen? It's quite simple.

Kanban is a simple framework that focuses on the use of pictorial and high quality painted spread across a board in order to a team to visualize and have a clear perception of what they had accomplished, what their challenges are, and what their target should be. Kanban is all about effectiveness and efficiency in a team. If the team possesses this amazing quality, then trust me, Kanban is the best methodology you can ever think of. It has a unique way of bringing loopholes to light no matter how hard they must have hidden.

You can also use so many cues in Kanban. Cues like the Kanban Boards which be used in holding the other tools of making a Kanban. It is more like the mother to all Kanban cues. The Kanban Cards are the working hands of the whole Kanban process. Each card depicts a different meaning so as not to confuse anyone in the team. This would aid communication and make everything clear. Then the Kanban Swimlanes are what would aid you in differentiating the tasks in the visual board. Be that as it may, this is what Kanban really entails.

4. Lean: This is another whole new discussion entirely. It would interest you to know that it has no connection with the Agile method. This methodology focuses on the end result which involves the customers and also tries to cut waste in any way that it can. Instead of having a large pool of resources at your disposal and end up having very limited resources, this methodology is the best method you can employ in order to come out with an amazing result.

This methodology is also gotten from one of the Japanese fastest growing industry, the manufacturing industry. With Lean, wastes are reduced, the quality will improve drastically, and the cost will also be reduced. That way, it going to be a win-win situation for everybody. There are three types of Lean methodology and they are Muda, Mura, and Muri. These can also be known as the 3Ms of Project Management.

Muda seeks to eliminate waste. This is the primary function of Muda. Anywhere it sees irrelevances, it cuts it off, especially if it doesn't add any value to the project. And when we are referring to wastes, we are talking about time wasting, resources wasting and so much more.

Mura also is all about elimination. But instead of focusing on wastes, it focuses its lens on the obstruction and variances present in the project. This would, in turn, give it the necessary flow it deserves for a successful Project. Then Muri is all about making sure the project stays afloat. It doesn't waste time in eliminating excess load and baggage the project is carrying.

5. Waterfall: The waterfall methodology had been in existence longer than many of the methodologies out there in the world of Project Management. It is a particular type of methodology which is designed in a downward slope. This downward slope is what will give you a waterfall shape at the end of your project design. This methodology was created by Winston W. Royce in his article of 1970.

This methodology focuses more on the documentation process. It deals with order in a project. For example, this methodology would give you the idea of making necessary arrangements where necessary. It would show you where you need to make adjustments. If one of your team members resigns, you will be able to fill in the new recruit through the documentation you've already filed out with the aid of this methodology. This type of methodology is also used in Software Project Management.

6. Six Sigma: The Six Sigma is a type of methodology that was first used in 1986 by the Motorola Company. A group of engineers came up with this methodology in order to improve the quality of their products and also to tackle the errors that may occur. The Six Sigma would help you identify possible problems that may affect your project by pointing towards the direction of every flaw. It might also involve statistics and empiricism. Thus, you will need people that are skilled in this method.

   There are different types of Six Sigma methodology and these are Six Sigma Green Belts and the Six Sigma Black Belts. These two types of Six Sigma are supervised by the Six Sigma Master Black Belts. There is also DMAIC and DMADV which are used in making sure the project goes smoothly. The Lean Six Sigma method would also help eliminate unnecessary waste.

Key Tools in Project Management.

1. Gantt Chart: This is one of the best scheduling tools you will ever find. It is easy to use and operate. Gantt Chart is a Project Management tool which can be used in showing the progress of each task and activity in a project. Developed in 1917, the Gantt Chart shows the priorities in the tasks as well as their connections. Ever since it

was introduced, it had become a driving force in today's world. The Gantt Chart was first used during the creation of America's Hoover Dam project of 1931. As a beginner in this line of professionalism, I would employ you to take this seriously as it would always come in handy.

2. 2. Logic Network: This is a certain network that shows the arrangements of activities and events during a specific time. That way, you will be able to foresee the next line of action in a project. This can also be used to identify the priorities in a project. The Logic Network will allow you to see things beforehand, that way, you will be able to predict the future and even tweak the project for a favorable outcome. This tool will even open your eyes to the possibilities around you. Additionally, important information would definitely surface no matter how hidden they may be.

3. PERT Chart: The Program Evaluation and Review Technique which is also known as PERT Chart is an important tool of Project Management created by the United States Department of Defense of the US Navy Special Projects Office. It was developed and formulated as a result of the Polaris mobile submarine-launched ballistic missile project which was carried out in the year 1958. The PERT Chart is similar to the Gantt

Chart. They both would tell you the exact that you can use to execute a task in a project.

4. Product Breakdown Structure (PBS): This is a tool of Project Management that shows the total connection and relationship of the products development and deliverables. The PBS comes in a kind of hierarchical tree or structure which seeks to point out the goals and objectives of the project. According to PBS, before developing a relationship as regards the product range, you should first make sure the structure is well grounded.

5. Work Breakdown Structure (WBS): Like the PERT Chart, the Work Breakdown Structure (WBS) is also one of the popular tools developed and created by the United States Development of Defense (DOD) all thanks to the Polaris mobile submarine-launched ballistic missile project in the year 1958. What the WBS seeks to do is to resize the deliverables so as to enable the tasks to be minimal in cost. The WBS is basically the base of every Project Planning.

In this chapter, we delved into the key techniques, methodologies, and tools which will come in handy during your projects. Whenever you feel your project is becoming difficult or complex, these techniques will help you move past that challenge. It will help you reach the desired destination. Additionally, you can mix them up or even use them one after the other. The choice is all yours. What should matter is the end result of the project. Additionally, there is no project without risk. No matter how little they may be, a risk is a risk. If not tackled appropriately, they might end up biting you in the butt. Thus, this is what the next chapter would talk about in details. Please turn over the page.

Chapter Eleven

Common Risks and Their Control.

There is no business without risk, neither is there any form of event, activities, strategy, and management without its own share of risks. In the same vein, Project Management is no saint in this line of classification. As a matter of fact, it's amazing and outstanding features which had made it universal all over the world also comes with its own blemish. No matter how hard you turn this, these risks are still probable circumstances that may occur along the line. However, knowing about them would give you a head-start as a beginner.

When you know what to expect, we will be able to turn the tides in our favor. This is what this chapter promises to unfold. Trust me, some projects are risk carriers in hiding. If you don't do your findings and study appropriately, you might not see the impending doom coming. This always happens to beginners who want to prove themselves in the labor market. No one will tell you if a project is risky. The client would want you to deal with every issue professional. That is why he or she is appointing you in the first place. But as a certified Project Manager, you should be able to tell if a certain project is risky or not.

Some project might not even show this at first. But along the line, you will start noticing different types of challenges coming up to frustrate your plans. Be that as it may, some projects are risky at the beginning and some are as a result of our decisions and actions. This is why we really need to check every decision and action, weigh out the pros and cons, and consult the team or client before taking it. Nevertheless, this chapter would help sensitize you with the common risks you will definitely face as a Project Manager, be it an expert or beginner. Risks know no master.

Either small or big, deep or shallow and simple or complex, risks can spoil our plans and drag our project back. It can even go a long way in destroying our plans. As a beginner, if you are faced with risk in your project, then do not panic. Panic won't solve the situation for you but instead, look closely at the situation and find ways in which you can turn the situation around for the better. Every twist and turn in a project comes with its own circumstances, thus, I will advise you to be very careful before making any decision. One wrong move and it's game over. Now, here are some of the common risk you will face while taking up a project.

1. Wrong Estimate: This happens all the time and as a beginner, it's definitely going to happen to you

too. Often times, the project gets stretched as a result of a miscalculated estimate of the amount of time for each schedule, the total amount of time the project will be executed, the amount of cost it would take for the project to be executed, the actual budget of the whole project, and so much more. When this happens, then you should know that your project would face a whole lot of challenges along the line. However, it's one of the common risks that may occur and you should watch out for.

Solution: I will recommend you choose someone very good at the estimate for this task. Not just everyone in the team is meant for this particular task. Additionally, with the new trend of AI, I will advise you not to slack off. Join the moving train and stay abreast with the trend. Make use of the different applications available today as they will make your work easy and efficient. And if the mistake is already made, then be fast about the solution. Don't let it drag for long before making the necessary adjustment.

2. Frequent change of goals and objectives. This is one annoying type of risk you might encounter along the line of your project. For example, the client might want to have a change of heart and decides he doesn't want the project to go a certain direction any longer. They would want

you to make the necessary adjustment without even looking at the cost and how much problem it would bring for you as the Project Manager. When this happens, what will you do as a Project Manager? How would you solve this problem?

Solution: Solving this is quite simple but very difficult at the same time. I know for a fact that the answers or solution to this problem lies in inculcating and infusing the necessary changes in the project but this comes with a price. For example, the project will even take more time to be completed, there would be another whole new round of calculations, every process would have to be revisited and at the same time tweaked to the desired form.

3. Unforeseen Circumstances: These are the type of risks we won't even see coming. They are there but we might not see them at first. But along the line, they will start showing themselves. It's better to prepare for these circumstances because they might end up spoiling your hard work. For example, a crucial member of your team might decide to travel or take a leave of absence, what if you don't or can't find a replacement almost immediately? This would definitely cost you and your project a whole lot.

Solution: Always make sure you have a backup plan before taking up a project while executing it and at the end of the project. This would come in handy, trust me. Thus, there would be no problem whatsoever when these problems occur. When these unforeseen circumstances showcase themselves, then the project would definitely get delayed, therefore, always be ready for the worst. That is the only way you would be able to overcome this problem and stay afloat with your project.

4. Risk of communication: A lot of Project Managers suffer from this particular risk all the time. I would like to stress the fact that on no circumstances should you imagine someone has gotten and understood your directives perfectly without having to repeat the directives over and over again. Remember that the project you will handle is delicate and should be handled with utmost concentration. Always make yourself clear. When they don't really understand you, they end up doing something wrong. This would affect your project sooner or later. Communication is the key to a successful Project, never forget that.

Solution: Always make sure you lay emphasis on your words when addressing your team either individually or generally. Make sure your words are crystal clear. This would reduce the rate of misunderstanding in the team. Make easy communication a priority in your team as this would make your team operate even better in the long run. Additionally, always create a mild atmosphere in the team. Be free to them and always tell them to come to you in cases of any misconception.

5. Overlooking design: Designs are there for a reason. They are the framework of the whole project. They showcase how best you can go about executing a project. In order words, pay close attention to the designs, they might help you point out loopholes in the project. However, a lot of expert Project Managers out there ends up overlooking the project designs and go with their instincts just to save time. Trust me, this might look cool but please don't emulate them as a beginner. Many of these experts end up making a mistake in the end. In order to save time, they tend to cut this process, thus, end up destroying their hard work.

Solution: Don't even try it. You might be lucky when you try it but the odds are greatly not in your favor. The Project design is part of the project for a reason, why not focus on it? Don't neglect it for no just reason and if you must, then be sure to know what you are doing.

6. Technical risks: This type of risks are also challenging as they come with their own level of disadvantages. For example, when the client cuts the budget of the project or decides to cut down the strength of your team, this would definitely affect your project one way or the other. You will now have to perform more functions, meet deadlines, and at the same time uphold the quality of your work.

Solution: Beforehand, I would recommend you learn how to work under unfavorable conditions. Remember, this ought to be one of your amazing superpowers as a Project Manager. You should also be able to multi-task. Thus, immerse yourself with all these attributes beforehand and work will be like play even in unfavorable conditions.

Risks may even come every day on the project. These may be tangible or mere ones. But when they come, do not panic. It's not the end of the world. Sometimes, these little ones sometimes come as a warning sign for the complex ones to come. Thus, I will advise you to stay prepared and ready to tackle them as they come. The next chapter would put the lid on our bottle of knowledge. You don't want to miss it.

Chapter Twelve

Tapping Into the realm of Possibilities

Well, there you have it, Project Management at your fingertips. Even the so-called topnotch Project Managers also began as a Beginner. However, with dedication, commitments, and perseverance, they triumph and moved up the food chain. This can be you if only you learn to start believing in yourself and also start practicing your skills in Project Management. You can now start using these management skills in your everyday life. A lot of people have this notion of Project Management being a professional skill. This is very wrong. Being a Project Manager also makes you a Life Project Management expert.

It is now up to you to start putting your life in order. With all the knowledge you have gotten from the beginning of this book, you should be able to perform the function of a Project Manager without much stress. Project Management is a very large field, thus, you should choose which area you would want to specialize in. This is better than wanting to focus on every aspect of the field. It might be to complex for you to handle.

Thus, focus your lens on any of the types of Project Management in order to come out as an expert in no time.

This book is a gift, use it wisely. And should in case you've already started your Project Management career and needed a kick in the butt, then this book can be your strong foot. Trust me, it will equip you with the necessary tools, methodologies, and techniques in which you would need in everyday Project Management. These topnotch Project Managers won't be nice. Don't think they will receive you with welcome hands just because you are new in the field. They will squeeze every ounce of opportunities that will come your way. They will compete with you for every possible project out there no matter how little.

Thus, I will urge you to be prepared. Make sure you are always ready for any competition whatsoever. Additionally, try and always boost your resume or portfolio in any way that you can. This would also come in handy. A Project Manager with a very strong portfolio finds it very easy to relate with clients and the team in general. Take that Management classes, either in person or online. Make sure you stay committed to building yourself in this field. Let every day count as you continuously strive towards developing and improving yourself with new experiences and knowledge.

And when the challenges come, remember that

there is no business without setbacks neither is there a project without challenges. Take them in good faith. That is the only way you can overturn the situation. In case you don't know how to overturn a certain challenge, then look for the situation inwardly. Search within yourself and look for what you are lacking as a Project Manager. Sometimes, Project Managers Sometimes, Project Managers often face the problem of not believing in their selves, thus, give up when the going gets tough. If these topnotch Project Managers had given up halfway, they wouldn't have been basking in the euphoria of success today.

Project Management is a trending line of professionalism today that will give you the career path that you seek. Aside from its amazing prospects and benefits, it comes with a particular type of joy which is derived from the organization, planning, and execution of projects. There is this particular joy that crept in when one is at the forefront of something productive. This is why many Project Managers out there perform their functions like it's nothing. When work becomes fun, the rest will become easy. If Project Management is your passion and you don't know how to go about it, then this book will help you through that phase.

In the end, you will be finally introduced into a world of Project Management. At the same time, you would be able to put your life in order and good shape. There would nothing you won't be able to handle. No matter how complex the event or activity might be, you will be able to make something meaningful out of it. Even if all the odds are against you, you will still be able to make something meaningful out of the situation. This is the goal of Project Management. It's not just about knowing how to use the experience and knowledge gotten on projects but to also apply it on everyday life. Life would definitely become bearable and meaningful.

As a Project Manager, you will be the to-go person. You will be the person everybody runs to in time of need and problem. You will be the fixer for everyone. In as much as the attention might get into your head, I will implore you not to forget the basics. Never forget to run a check or study on the project before embarking on it. The risks would always be there, don't overlook any of them. Make sure you are familiar with the kind of risk you will encounter in the course of the project. That way, you will be able to plan ahead and make necessary arrangement in tackling them when the need arises.

Also, your team isn't mannequins, they are your shadow. Make good use of them as they are there for a reason and that is to make your work easy and faster. Always consult them when you feel there is a need for that. Wherever you are not sure or clear, be free to call those vast in the area to make it clear. You are the head, thus, any wrong move you make will definitely affect the whole team and vice versa. Thus, always check with the team before deciding on an important decision. Know that each team member is a specialist in a particular aspect. Therefore, be sure to share the task according to their skills.

Go out to the world and establish yourself as a topnotch Project Manager in the making. Ripple by ripple, you will definitely attain your dream in this field of professionalism. All you need to do is to be patient and confident. Show how much you've learned and how much output you are willing to give to your clients and stakeholders. Additionally, hold your client close. You don't want to be seen as incompetent on your first project. That will reflect very badly on your resume. And remember first impression matters in this line of business. Make sure you sweep them off their feet completely at the first meeting. This would make them go soft on you.

And one thing about project management is that your clients get to call you back for a project when they feel you are capable of. Thus, the first impression is all you need. Do that and your name would be on the lips of every Project Manager in the country. It would only be a matter of time before you go international.

And that wraps it up on how to become a Project Manager. This process is no joke. It is not as easy as it sounds. In fact, it requires lots of hard work, perseverance, and skill in order for a beginner to move up the food chain in this line of professionalism. Nevertheless, I believe you will attain that position, all you need to do is just to believe in yourself and your potentials. The sky would be your starting point afterward.

Conclusion

Without mincing many words, this has been an amazing journey all through the chapters. In the end, I am certain you must have gotten the answers you are certain for. And if you still haven't gotten your answers as regards Project Management, then I will suggest you look inward. Look closely at yourself and point out how you feel. Remember, Project Management and Emotional Intelligence goes hand in hand. Go for emotional intelligence classes if you must. It would help you contain your feelings and make you feel better afterward.

You can't be the amazing Project Manager you had always dreamed of if you don't get your act together. First, you need to have a clear mind to make that happen. Be that as it may, go out there and make history. Go out there and make a name for yourself. After all, this is why you have been focused, committed, and patient.

Now, let's do a quick recap, shall we? In case you had forgotten what our chapters looked like, chapter one delved into the historical background of Project Management. Questions like how did Project Management come into being? Who and why was Project Management coined? And so much more were answered in this chapter. Chapter two of this book also defined Project Management along with the key concepts associated with it. We can go into Project Management without taking a walk into this line of thought. The chapter highlighted scholarly definitions as well as that of the concepts.

Chapter three focuses its lens on how one can become a Project Manager. This is one of the reasons why a lot of you had picked up this book. Make sure you pay close attention to the chapter as it explains everything in general. Chapter four also looked at the duties, roles, and functions of a Project Manager. The role of a Project Manager goes beyond just managing. This chapter shows you that as it sheds more light on what it takes to be a real Project Manager. Chapter five will show you tips on how to be successful in this field of professionalism. You might want to start infusing to your everyday endeavors.

Chapter six looked at the common mistakes you might make as a beginner. Mistakes have no master, thus, don't feel bad as even the best in this field make mistakes too. Chapter seven also holds something interesting. It will sensitize you on the new trends and also focus on the kinds of trends we have in today's world. You don't want to be left out. Chapter eight also delved into Project plan and to go about making an amazing plan for the success of your project. If I were you, I will utilize this gift appropriately. Chapter nine contains Project Control. If you don't have this, then you are not fit to be a Project Manager. This chapter would teach you how to gain control of your project.

And chapter ten, eleven, and twelve looks at the key techniques, methodologies, & tools, common risks, and their control, and tapping into the realm of possibilities respectively. These chapters would further broaden your horizon in more ways you can ever think of. With that being said, it's left for you to make use of what you had assimilated so far. All I can tell you now is good luck and thank you for sticking with us this far.

All the best and God bless!

www.ingramcontent.com/pod-product-compliance
Lightning Source LLC
Chambersburg PA
CBHW071503080526
44587CB00014B/2196